NEW MERMAIDS

D1037697

John Vanbrugh

The
Relapse

or VIRTUE IN DANGER

edited by Bernard Harris

University of York

Bloomsbury Methuen Drama

An imprint of Bloomsbury Publishing Plc

50 Bedford Square	1385 Broadway
London	New York
WC1B 3DP	NY 10018
UK	USA

www.bloomsbury.com

Bloomsbury is a registered trade mark of Bloomsbury Publishing Plc

First New Mermaid edition published 1971
By Ernest Benn Limited

© Ernest Benn Limited 1971

Visit www.bloomsbury.com to find out more about our authors and their books
You will find extracts, author interviews, author events and you can sign up for
newsletters to be the first to hear about our latest releases and special offers.

British Library Cataloguing-in-Publication Data
A catalogue record for this book is available from the British Library.

ISBN: PB:	978-0-7136-2887-6
EPDF:	978-1-4081-4509-8
EPUB:	978-1-4081-4510-4

Library of Congress Cataloging-in-Publication Data
A catalog record for this book is available from the Library of Congress.

The
Relapse

NEW MERMAIDS

NEW MERMAIDS

General editors: William C. Carroll, Boston University
Brian Gibbons, University of Münster
Tiffany Stern, University of Oxford

The interior of a Restoration theatre
drawn by C.Walter Hodges

J. Miller Sc.

CONTENTS

.

TO

J. Amanda S.

ACKNOWLEDGEMENTS

LIKE ANY other modern student of Vanbrugh I am indebted to the work of two men in particular, Laurence Whistler for *Sir John Vanbrugh, Architect and Dramatist* (1938), and *The Imagination of Vanbrugh and his fellow artists* (1954), and Bonamy Dobrée, for *Restoration Comedy* (1924), and (with G. Webb) for *The Complete Works of Sir John Vanbrugh*, 4 vols. (1927–28).

My introduction and commentary have drawn upon these works, together with the edition of D. MacMillan and H. M. Jones (1931) and that of G. H. Nettleton and A. E. Case (1939); C. A. Zimansky's edition, though it arrived too late for full appreciation, is clearly a most valuable account of the play. I am grateful to Dr C. A. Patrides for providing me with a transcript of *Words for the Musick, in The Relapse: or, Vertue in Danger* (?1708), BM 806.K.16.(68+).

I must also record my thanks to the Librarians of the Universities of York and of Leeds for their practical assistance. And in addition to the revival of *The Relapse* at The Phoenix Theatre in 1947 I should like to acknowledge the pleasurable insight into Vanbrugh provided by two other productions, Toby Robertson's production of *The Confederacy* for the touring Prospect Company, at the Georgian Theatre, Richmond, 1964, and Donald Bodley's production of *Virtue in Danger*, at The Theatre Royal, York, 1966.

B. A. H.

York,
May 1971

INTRODUCTION

THE AUTHOR

JOHN VANBRUGH was christened on 24 January 1664 at his father's house in the parish of St Nicholas Acon, London.[1] Vanbrugh was the ninth child and first surviving son of the nineteen children of Giles and Elizabeth Vanbrugh. His Flemish grandfather, Gillis van Brugg of Ghent, had fled from Alva's religious persecution, married an Englishwoman, and presumably become sufficiently established in the world of London merchant enterprise for his son Giles to marry Elizabeth Barker, daughter of Sir Dudley Carleton, the nephew of the famous statesman Lord Dorchester. Vanbrugh's Flemish ancestry was not without distinction, and when he applied to the College of Heralds for confirmation of his coat-of-arms he was able to summon up in his support a Praetor of Ypres from 1383.[2]

For so prominent and public a man as Vanbrugh the records of his life are often tantalisingly incomplete, yet they at least offer a possible framework for reasonable speculation. By 1667 his father was established as a sugar-baker in Chester, where it is assumed that John was educated. At the age of twenty-two he was commissioned in the Earl of Huntingdon's Foot Regiment, but resigned his commission in August of the same year. He received a competence at his father's death in July 1689. Presumably he was intended for a military career, but the next phase of Vanbrugh's career is obscured by uncertainty as to the nature of his military service. He was arrested in France in 1688, imprisoned at Calais in 1690, transferred at his own cost to Vincennes in 1691, and early in 1692 was imprisoned in the Bastille.[3] In November of that year he was paroled and came home. It is assumed that he was used in the game of bartering prisoners.

After a brief spell as an auditor for the Southern Division of Lancaster he was again commissioned in Lord Berkeley's Marine

[1] The main materials for a biography are contained in Bonamy Dobrée's *Essays in Biography* (1925), and in his Introduction to Dobrée and Webb, *The Complete Works of Sir John Vanbrugh*, 4 vols. (1927–28), Vol. I.
[2] A genealogical table for Vanbrugh's immediate family is provided in the preface to A. E. H. Swain's edition of Vanbrugh in the Mermaid Series (1896), but it needs correction and deserves amplification.
[3] See A. Rosenberg, 'New light on Vanbrugh', *Philological Quarterly*, 1966.

Regiment of Foot in 1696, and by 1702 was a captain in a regiment raised by his first commander, the Earl of Huntingdon.

By that date, however, like his contemporaries Captain Steele and Captain Farquhar, Vanbrugh had already commenced as playwright, and unlike them, had begun a second career as an architect. Military service, in those days, was not only compatible with other employments but the means of preferment to them. Vanbrugh's most secure social asset, however, was probably simply his personality; he was known 'upon the town' as Captain Vanbrugh, but to a more intimate circle of acquaintances as 'Brother Van'; above all he was a clubman in an age exceptionally devoted to such fraternities, and a member of one of the most influential societies of the day, the Kit Cat club, founded by Vanbrugh's life-long friend, Jacob Tonson the printer.

It seems entirely in character that Vanbrugh's first completed play was undertaken partly in order to pay off a debt and partly to help out a friend. For according to Colley Cibber when Vanbrugh was 'but an ensign, and had a heart above his income' he had been helped financially by Sir Thomas Skipwith, a patentee of the Theatre Royal, Drury Lane. In 1695, Thomas Betterton—the foremost actor of the day—quarrelled with Christopher Rich, the manager of the Theatre Royal, and left, together with many of the company, to work at the new theatre in Lincoln's Inn Fields. Faced with a crisis of an unusual scale, Colley Cibber wrote *Love's Last Shift* in 1696 to reinstate the surviving company at the Theatre Royal, and Vanbrugh dashed off, in six weeks, *The Relapse, or Virtue in Danger*, first performed in November 1696, and the success of the following season. In December was performed the first part of Vanbrugh's adaptation of Boursault's *Les Fables d'Esope* as *Aesop*. Vanbrugh forwent his profits on these two plays, and presumably met his obligation to Skipwith. *The Relapse* had brought him instant notoriety and his pen was soon in demand for the rival company. Charles Montagu, a prominent Kit Cat, later Earl of Halifax and a Chancellor of the Exchequer, persuaded Vanbrugh to revise the comedy he was said to have drafted while in the Bastille, and the result was *The Provok'd Wife*, performed at Lincoln's Inn Fields in April 1697, with Betterton as Sir John Brute and Mrs Barry in the title role. The calculated affront to morality given in the preface to the printed edition of *The Relapse* was now substantially extended, and in 1698 Vanbrugh and Congreve were arraigned in Jeremy Collier's *A Short View of the Immorality and Profaneness of the English Stage*.

The Collier controversy is one of the most famous and complex of such recurrent events in English theatre history and can only be dealt with here in a few matters that particularly concern Vanbrugh.

Collier and Vanbrugh were so opposite in character and in outlook that there was really a state of no contest between them rather than the grounds of difference. Collier was what Laurence Whistler has called 'an example of that curious and undesirable type, the high-church Puritan'.[4] He was officially an outlaw, having been associated with some unsavoury activities, such as the scaffold benedictions he helped to conduct at the execution of some Jacobite rebels. He was stung into attack upon Vanbrugh partly by the latter's contemptuous prediction of from what quarter he could expect hostile criticism, for in the preface to *The Relapse* he lampooned his likely castigator as a man with 'flat plod shoes, a little band, greasy hair, and a dirty face'. This preface, though it antedates the actual controversy, remains Vanbrugh's most vigorous and entertaining statement of his case. By comparison his *A short vindication of 'The Relapse' and 'The Provok'd Wife' from Immorality and Prophaneness* (1698) makes the disappointing mistake of fighting on Collier's prepared ground. Collier's whole case grew and flourished from the stony soil of his belief that 'The business of Plays is to recommend Virtue and dis-countenance Vice'. And when Vanbrugh fell, surprisingly heavily, for this line of cant, he had little alternative but to pass off his intentions as didactic. Collier's main charges against Vanbrugh were that he wrote bawdy, blasphemous, and dramatically incompetent plays. The first charge might be accepted with the kind of positive welcome we extend to Shakespeare's achievement in that sphere, and as Whistler points out, the more serious matter of the exploitation of children then fashionable on the Restoration stage was not one to which Vanbrugh was an accomplice; again the blasphemy was trivial, and largely depended upon the dissenting Vanbrugh's attitude to the hypocrisy of clergymen, perhaps more evident then than at most future dates; the accusation of technical inefficiency in the composition of plays is more interesting, because at least argu-able, and will be referred to later in discussing the construction of *The Relapse*. What made Collier's attack serious for the dramatists was not its polemical strength so much as its popular appeal. The theatre had become dangerously divisive in social terms, and there was political capital to be made from the calculated affront to middle-class susceptibilities. Collier became the voice of a long-lived philistinism, and as Whistler comments:

> The desire for such a movement no doubt existed already, but Collier made it articulate. And so he must be ranked with Addison among those who, in the realm of behaviour, helped to kill the age of Baroque and introduce the age of Sentiment.[5]

[4] *Sir John Vanbrugh, Architect and Dramatist, 1664–1726* (1938), p. 41.
[5] ibid., p. 47.

It is sometimes argued that Vanbrugh's career as a playwright was affected by Collier's onslaught, since his future work—apart from the unfinished *A Journey to London*—consisted of adaptations. It seems more credible, however, that the demands of his new career as an architect became increasingly absorbing of his energy. In 1698 he had adapted Dancourt's farce *La Maison de Campagne* as *The Country House*, very successfully indeed; but his thoughts were already turning to real participation in the making of the English country house. In 1699 he drew up plans for a new house for the Earl of Carlisle, a fellow Kit Cat member, and twice First Lord of the Treasury. His ideas were accepted and he was appointed architect. In 1702, with Carlisle's support, he became Comptroller of the Board of Works, in 1703 he was appointed Carlisle Herald, and in 1704 Clarenceux King-of-Arms. Naturally such success led to bitterness among his professional rivals, perhaps made more extreme by the typically derisive manner with which he had written of the earnest study of genealogy in *Aesop*. Yet Whistler's observation deserves respect: 'No other Englishman ever made such an entry into the art.'[6] Vanbrugh's genius had finally found its most effective form of expression.

Even so, Vanbrugh did not immediately desert the theatre. Indeed, his ambitions for it outran its capacity for response. In 1700 he adapted Fletcher's *The Pilgrim*, for which Dryden wrote a prologue, epilogue, and the incomparable *A Secular Masque*: and in 1701 he adapted Dancourt's version of Rojas Zorrilla's *The False Friend* for Drury Lane. In 1703 he tried to unite his interests by purchasing a site in the Haymarket for a future new theatre to be run by Congreve and himself for a company led by Betterton. In 1704 he collaborated with Congreve and Walsh in a translation of Molière's *Monsieur de Pourceaugnac* for Lincoln's Inn Fields. But though the Queen's Theatre, or Italian Opera House, opened in 1705 under the joint management of Vanbrugh and Congreve, events were already moving against Vanbrugh's further participation in the world of theatre. Marlborough's victory at Blenheim in 1704 had immediate consequences for Vanbrugh, who was appointed Surveyor for the building of Blenheim Palace in 1705. In the same year he provided a brilliant adaptation of Dancourt's *Les Bourgeoises à la Mode* as *The Confederacy*, and a weaker version of Molière's *Le Dépit Amoureux* as *The Mistake*, but his commitments as architect were already onerous enough, even without the inevitable additional problems of dealing with the Duchess of Marlborough.

The next decade contained mingled fortune and misfortune for Vanbrugh. In 1706, by a preferment which further antagonised his

⁶ ibid., p. 49.

political rivals, he went to Hanover to invest the future King George I with the Order of the Garter, and the moment must have seemed to Vanbrugh the triumph of his own political ambition, which was that shared by members of the Kit Cat club, namely to secure the Hanoverian succession. Vanbrugh's reward came in 1714 when he was the first knight created on George's accession. But long before that date the penalties of social and political success were being demanded. Defoe, in the *Review* of 3 May 1705, perhaps began the attack, which was continued in *The Rehearsal of Observator* of 5 May 1705 in which the Queen's Theatre was skilfully satirised:

> The Kit-Cat Club is now grown Notorious all over the Kingdom. And they have built a Temple for their Dagon, the new Play-House in the Hay-Market.

Vanbrugh, preceded by Congreve, began to withdraw from the venture into theatre-management, and though he persuaded the Duke of Manchester, another Kit Cat member, to introduce Handel into England, their concern for opera was premature. Ambiguities in the contract for Blenheim Palace, intended by the government as a national monument for Marlborough, led to protracted disputes over payment, and Vanbrugh was only rescued by the intervention of another Kit Cat companion, Robert Walpole. The relationship between Queen Anne and the Duchess of Marlborough deteriorated alarmingly and Vanbrugh was caught up in a battle of personalities at least as exhausting as engagement in formal politics. In 1716 he resigned from the Surveyorship of Blenheim, and though his career was fully devoted to architecture thereafter, the strain of those arguments seems to have sapped even his prodigious energy.

On 14 January 1719 he married Henrietta Maria Yarborough, a daughter of James Yarborough of Heslington Hall, York, former Lieutenant-Colonel of Horse and aide-de-camp to Marlborough, at St Lawrence's Church, York. Vanbrugh was then fifty-five, his wife twenty-six. Gossip naturally attended their courtship[7] and misfortune their marriage: Vanbrugh wrote to the Duke of Newcastle on 11 August 1719 about 'a bit of a girle popping into the world three months before its time'. Charles, their only child to survive infancy, died of wounds at the battle of Fontenoy in 1745. Long before that, however, Vanbrugh himself had died of a quinzey, on 26 March 1726, to be buried in the family vault of St Stephen Walbrook's, a church built by his old master Sir Christopher Wren.

Vanbrugh's widow, whom he evidently and eloquently loved, survived him by exactly half a century. He left behind him an unfinished play, *A Journey to London*, which cannot be dated but which

[7] See *Letters and Works of Lady Mary Wortley Montagu* (1837), Vol. I, 155.

seems from its style to be the latest and most accomplished of his writings for the stage. It was completed by Colley Cibber as *The Provok'd Husband*, and was a long-standing success. The irony of this fact is scarcely tolerable. For the direction of English comedy which Vanbrugh sought to prevent when he adapted the sentimentality of Cibber's *Love's Last Shift* into the realism of *The Relapse*, was totally subverted by Cibber's betrayal of Vanbrugh's intentions in terms of sentimental comedy. Vanbrugh, in fact, fought a losing battle, both as a comic dramatist and as an architect. Kenneth Muir has observed:

> The success of Collier's diatribe was bad enough; the applause which greeted *Love's Last Shift* was worse, and it adumbrated the triumph of sentimental comedy.[8]

Vanbrugh's achievements as an architect—supported by Hawksmoor and dependent upon the genius of Wren—were not to be recognised in an age dominated by the aesthetic dogmas of Burlington and the neo-classicists. Reynolds redeemed Vanbrugh's architecture in due course, in his Thirteenth Discourse of 11 December 1786, and his judgment has been supported.[9] But no modern critic has succeeded in commanding the understanding of Vanbrugh's art of comedy so completely as those critics who, for a brief moment, enjoyed both a sympathy for his age and an intelligible and communicable delight in his comic genius, Leigh Hunt and William Hazlitt.[10]

Admittedly, his political enemies paid their overdue respects after his death; thus Swift and Pope apologised in their *Miscellanies* of 1727:

> In Regard to Two Persons only we wish our Railery, though ever so tender, or Resentment, though ever so just, had not been indulged. We speak of Sir John Vanbrugh, who was a Man of Wit, and of

---

[8] *The Comedy of Manners* (1970), p. 125.

[9] Boswell, in *The Life of Samuel Johnson* (dedicated to Sir Joshua Reynolds), paid a tribute which Vanbrugh would have appreciated:

'In the Life of Blackmore, we find that writer's reputation generously cleared by Johnson from the cloud of prejudice which the malignity of contemporary wits had raised around it. In this spirited exertion of justice, he has been imitated by Sir Joshua Reynolds, in his praise of the architecture of Vanbrugh.' (*Boswell's Life of Johnson*, Oxford edition, 1927, 2 vols. in I, Vol. II, 372.)

[10] Hazlitt's observations are in his *Lectures on the English Comic Writers* (1819): the relevant passages from Leigh Hunt's *The Dramatic Works of Wycherley, Congreve, Vanbrugh and Farquhar* (1875) are given in Swain's edition mentioned above.

Honour, and of Mr Addison, whose Name deserves all Respect from every Lover of Learning.

The tribute, though comfortably posthumous, of Swift and Pope, is perhaps more valued support than that afforded by modern literary critics in any proferred defence and advocacy of Vanbrugh as a comic dramatist.

THE PLAY

Cibber wrote *Love's Last Shift, or The Fool in Fashion* with the double intention of attracting a new audience for a different kind of comedy and of providing himself with a substantial part. He was doubly successful, his play being recommended to the patentees by Southerne and receiving immediate recognition as an original development in comedy, and his acting as Sir Novelty Fashion established him—he was then twenty-four—among the leading actors of the day.

When Vanbrugh undertook the sequel he made a sceptical use of several of the elements of Cibber's play and had the important benefit that some of the main parts continued to be played by the same actors and actresses; Cibber reappeared as Lord Foppington, Verbruggen as Loveless, and Mrs Rogers as Amanda; Mrs Verbruggen who had played the pert minor part of Narcissa was given a major role as Berinthia, a much more significant foil to Amanda than Cibber had provided with Hillaria and Narcissa.

Cibber's play dealt mainly with the reconciliation of the caddish Loveless, a debtor and deserter, to his forgiving, virtuous wife; the comic relief from the strains of sentiment was largely dispensed by the absurdities of Sir Novelty's self-preoccupation with the role of a beau. In some ways Cibber was continuing a pattern of social comedy glancing at contemporary manners, but in a more important respect he was consciously steering the line of his plot in a calculated artifice to create a new, sentimental, and contrived ending, with the rake reformed and the marriage relationship restored, a situation which depended for its theatrical effect less upon the plausibility of Cibber's handling of character as upon an evocation of Shakespeare's *All's Well that Ends Well*.

Since Vanbrugh is so often censured for his morals, or lack of them, it is worth pointing out the cynicism with which Cibber commented upon his own strategy in the conduct of *Love's Last Shift*; Miss Cross said in the epilogue:

> Such out-of-fashion stuff! But then again,
> He's lewd for above four acts, gentlemen!

> For, faith, he knew, when once he'd changed his fortune
> And reformed his vice, 'twas time to drop the curtain.
> Four acts for your coarse palates was designed,
> But then the ladies' taste is more refined;
> They, for Amanda's sake, will sure be kind.

If one remembers the clever appeal to the ladies in the prologue of Shakespeare's and Fletcher's *Henry VIII* then one must recognise how far Cibber was prepared to fall in attracting a new audience at a time of similar theatrical conditions.

Vanbrugh would have none of this false appeal to an alleged feminine sensibility. He did not believe in the easy reformation of Loveless, nor perhaps in allowing Amanda to represent, uncriticised, a feminine ideal. He switched the name of Worthy in Cibber's play to a new creation of his own, a libertine in pursuit of Amanda (so that she had real temptation to contend with) and in league with Berinthia, so that several possibilities for confidences, confusion, and collusion were ready made, in the way of the town. Vanbrugh braced this single plot with a second one, playing off, as Shadwell had done before him, provincial life against town life, and not only in the conversation of the metropolitan society[11] but in location too. Young Fashion, younger brother to Lord Foppington, having failed to come by any of Foppington's ten thousand pounds inheritance, accepts Coupler's plot to impersonate his brother and so obtains the hand of Hoyden, daughter of Sir Tunbelly Clumsey, an heiress of £1,500 a year. The plot is successful eventually only because of the culpable and acquisitive natures of Bull, Sir Tunbelly's chaplain, and Hoyden's Nurse.

What relates these two plots is not so much the pivotal role of Lord Foppington, repulsed by Amanda and cheated by his brother, as the extent to which Vanbrugh offers self-interest, sexual appetite, and social ambition as governing so many relationships. Thus Loveless's initial motive for his eventual relapse is a desire to return to that social world where he has already proved himself unable to avoid temptation. By chance the object of his current

---

[11] Mr Ron Clayton has drawn my attention to the following reference by J. P. Kenyon to the 'court tune', an 'affected nasal drawl', which Sunderland may have 'adopted to hide some impediment of speech': 'As an example of this "court tune", take his remark on the new privy council of April 1679: "Whaat . . . if his Majesty taarn out faarty of us, may not he have faarty athors to saarve him as well? And whaat maaters who saarves his Majesty, so lang as his Majesty is saarved?" ' Roger North, *Examen* (1740), 77. The Earl of Ailesbury also mentions his 'unusual drawling tone', *Memoirs* (1890), i, 303. See J. P. Kenyon, *Robert Spencer, Earl of Sunderland 1641–1702* (1958), p. 330 and note.

fascination turns out to be Amanda's cousin, the sophisticated and widowed Berinthia, whom Amanda presses to live with them. In her wake, in turn, comes Worthy, attracted to Amanda. Upon them next calls Foppington, presuming upon his recent elevation to the peerage to attempt the quick conquest of Amanda. She is thus exposed much more strenuously than in Cibber's play both to social pressure and to personal dilemma: she finds it easy to repulse Foppington's confident impertinence, but she is cruelly placed when Berinthia becomes her confidant in trying to deal with Worthy.

From this claustrophobic world anticipating Richardson, Vanbrugh rescues us with an invigorating chase that looks forward to Fielding. Young Fashion sets off in pursuit of an heiress, and the sport is made entertaining by the co-operative nature of the quarry. For Hoyden is not an innocent country miss, but a high-spirited seeker after town life. She does not mind whom she marries if her future husband can provide her with a London home and open to her the glittering world of social success and future conquests. What makes such behaviour amusing rather than distressing is that Vanbrugh has taken care to deprive Hoyden of a mother. To her father, the cheerful, insensitive, and wholly gross Sir Tunbelly Clumsey, Hoyden is merely the means to possible social advancement. If she can marry a lord then her dowry will have been well spent. To her Nurse Hoyden is a creature of merely animal relationship; as she tells Young Fashion:

> all I can boast of is, I gave her pure good milk, and so your honour would have said, an you had seen how the poor thing sucked it.— Eh, God's blessing on the sweet face on't! how it used to hang at this poor teat, and suck and squeeze, and kick and sprawl it would, till the belly on't was so full, it would drop off like a leech.
>
> HOYDEN (*To* NURSE, *taking her angrily aside*)
> Pray one word with you. Prithee nurse, don't stand ripping up old stories, to make one ashamed before one's love. Do you think such a fine proper gentleman as he cares for a fiddlecome tale of a draggle-tailed girl? If you have a mind to make him have a good opinion of a woman, don't tell him what one did then, tell him what one can do now.—(*To* YOUNG FASHION) I hope your honour will excuse my mismanners to whisper before you; it was only to give some orders about the family.   (IV, i, 82–96)

In her own way Hoyden is protected by Vanbrugh, just as Amanda is protected, by his delineation of the social context in which both are presented. Hoyden and Amanda are not really loved by those who have immediate responsibility for them. They make their own way in the muddled moral environment which surrounds them. Hoyden develops a tough, if inexperienced, attitude towards the married state, directly responsive to her father's cynicism. Amanda, bleakly aware of the actualities, still clings to the ideal possibilities. In these relationships, between Hoyden and her Nurse and Amanda and Berinthia, Vanbrugh is close to those understandings generated by Shakespeare in his depiction of the relationships between Juliet and her Nurse and Desdemona and Emilia. This is not to claim for Vanbrugh Shakespeare's power in presenting human relationships, but only to note that in such instances the cynicism bred of worldly experience counterbalances the immaturity and trust without ridiculing them.

The great strength of *The Relapse* lies in the play's sheer vivacity, whether in language or action. Its dialogue is written with natural ease, and though it lacks the intellectual wit of many comedies of manners, this is partly because, Foppington apart, it is less concerned with affectations of behaviour than with naturalness of character. The dramatic rhythm of the play, the swift pulse of its plotting, has a comparable directness. Such matters are part of the play's very obviously masculine appeal, and its uninhibited indulgence of physical appetite brought about immediate censure and subsequent bowdlerisation; yet its unrestrained freedom of speech and action is essential to its stage life. It is for these qualities that the play has been re-appreciated in recent years, and not because our age has become as 'permissive' as that of Vanbrugh's day, but because the way in which Vanbrugh entertains us is ultimately persuasive of the real affection, neither ideal nor sentimental, with which he views his created beings. Vanbrugh's opinion of humanity is an exuberant compound of cynicism and generosity, and possibly his own standpoint is nearest to that displayed by Worthy; self-interest is usually uppermost, but it has the capacity to acknowledge higher values and to give way.

Such generalisations about *The Relapse* may suggest an over-sentimental judgment, a claim that Vanbrugh was moral despite himself. Yet if we do try to treat of the charges against Vanbrugh, that in this play he offended deliberately against accepted social morality, a case can surely be made that rather, in a largely farcical fashion, he presented contemporary conduct with a frankness and acceptance which delighted as much as it shocked. Indeed, one may take a positive line about the argument over Vanbrugh's immorality, and ask, who is corrupted by the behaviour of his characters, and who, among his characters, is corrupted? Collier thought there was an especial immorality in the way in which Young Fashion was doubly rewarded for his deceit, but this example has to be seen in full context. Let us review the major offences which the play commits against accepted morality.

Most seriously, Loveless betrays Amanda by seducing Berinthia; Young Fashion betrays his brother by deceitfully marrying Hoyden. There is no question that these events offend against general morality; but how do they stand in the personal morality of those involved? Loveless, as his name implies, is an emotionally weak character, whose inconsistency was so established a fact that Vanbrugh could not accept Cibber's depiction of his conversion to constancy. Loveless remains the moral failure that Amanda knows him to be. Berinthia selfishly accepts Loveless, but in doing so deprives Amanda of nothing that she really possesses, for Loveless's constancy has never been something which she could command. Amanda, as Vanbrugh sees her, learns far more about her relationship with Loveless than she ever could in Cibber's protective scheme. For in her conversations with Berinthia she raises many questions which reflect upon her understanding of herself, and what is most remarkable in their intimate discussion in V, ii is that Berinthia proves more loyal to Amanda's own sense of herself than to her own opportunist sense of triumph: Amanda, though cuckolded, is never ridiculed, and she has more dignity in Vanbrugh's presentation than in Cibber's. Indeed, through the discovery of her own powers of envy, and particularly through being offered by Worthy a chance of personal revenge, she develops a much more impressive sensibility than that granted her by Cibber. In some respects she is a character drawn again in Vanbrugh's finest creation, Lady Brute, where self-knowledge is sooner attained and more poignantly expressed. Yet Amanda is already a fully realised person, just as *The Relapse*, as a whole, does not depend upon Cibber's play, but is already a separate study of human characters.

Young Fashion's betrayal of Lord Foppington is less serious, and on two counts, social and personal. Young Fashion attracts much of the sympathy awarded to a younger brother of his class for the two centuries or more in which such a plight was recognisable. His humiliation at the hands of Lord Foppington when he requests a financial share in the latter's new fortune does not justify his behaviour, any more than Hoyden's willingness to marry the first-comer condones it. Yet there is a deeper psychological motivation which confirms the rightness of the union between Young Fashion and Hoyden: simply, Lord Foppington does not need, financially or emotionally, to enter into an arranged marriage; whereas Young Fashion and Hoyden accept each other on sight, however mis-guidedly on her part or cynically on his, and their mutual acceptance draws its fittingness from the fact that they serve each other's needs; for her, freedom from domestic tyranny, for him, financial freedom from social servitude. Indeed, Young Fashion and Hoyden arrive at such an understanding of themselves that there remains a reasonable hope that they will contrive a fashionable marriage on rather better terms, that is, in terms of social acceptability, than would have been the case if she had married Lord Foppington. The possibility that she will revert to that intended state is, of course, left open at the end of the play, in its outrageous conclusion; but the possible profligacy has already been undercut by the hint of the actual compatibility of Young Fashion and Hoyden.

To argue thus, about the personal morality of individual characters, is perhaps to protest too much against established opinion. Yet even in Vanbrugh's most depraved character, Coupler, there is a magnanimity of nature which reflects the life-affirming quality of the whole play. Coupler, though a homosexual, is a professional marriage-arranger. Yet he acts, in contriving Young Fashion's successful defeat of Lord Foppington, on the side of youth, vigour, and natural lust. His real reward could not be merely financial; it would be Young Fashion's acceptance of him. He is repulsed at once:

COUPLER
Ha! you young lascivious rogue, you. Let me put my hand in your bosom, sirrah.
FASHION
Stand off, old Sodom!   (I, iii, 181–3)

There is even the distinct possibility, since Young Fashion was played originally by Mrs Kent, in the 'breeches part' later established as a pantomime convention, that Coupler's interest in Young Fashion was cruelly mistaken from the start; the important point, however, is that he does not bear malice; he carries out his part in the plot on the side of what seems to him to be personal and social justice; in enforcing the marriage of Bull and the Nurse he even acts in terms of social convention, by regularising their union.

At this point the strain of presenting Vanbrugh as a promoter of orthodox morality must be admitted. But before surrendering the position, something must be said in answer to Collier's strongest charge, that Vanbrugh wrote not blank verse but 'Fustian' when attempting to deal with serious emotional matters. There is certainly a case to be answered. Kenneth Muir has observed that

Cibber, whether accidentally or by design, drops into blank verse in emotional passages; and the same thing . . . is apt to happen with Vanbrugh and Farquhar.[12]

The phenomenon is very evident in *The Relapse*, but it cannot, of course, be exonerated readily. Curt Zimansky makes the interesting comment that Vanbrugh's

[12] op. cit., p. 127.

choice of verse for scenes of sentiment may owe something to
Cibber's rhythmic prose, but he also avails himself of a tradition in
Restoration drama of quite irregular blank verse (Aphra Behn's
The Rover offers good examples) which allows him to write verse
lines without the obligation that they scan.[13]

So far as I know Zimansky is the only critic to raise the theatrical
point that Vanbrugh chose to indicate the emotional state of his
characters by use of an ambiguous form of language, since 'we are
apt to take the dubious verse as one more indication that the emotions
are forced.' But, while acknowledging the possibility, Zimansky mentions as a scene of crucial difficulty that between Amanda and
Worthy (V, iv), where the early texts print verse degenerating into
prose and recovering momentarily. Although I can well see that
Vanbrugh's manuscript presented the compositor with severe
problems, it remains a possibility that copy was followed, since, in
the only professional performance of this scene I have witnessed, the
actor playing Worthy was able to use these fluctuations of form
naturally, to suggest an artifice in his first formal approach, followed
by an eagerness which disrupted such formality, and succeeded by
an exhibition of heroics which broke up the language patterns entirely; the attack upon the structure of the language led to a further
relief, and the soliloquy which concludes the scene was spoken
naturally, or prosaically. I do not think Vanbrugh calculated matters
in this way: he claimed that he wrote as he spoke, and Cibber
reported that actors found 'the style of no author whatsoever gave
their memory less trouble'. Yet Cibber's remark is so often quoted
out of its full context, as a patronising comment upon the ease of
Vanbrugh's style, that the remark deserves to be given its full weight:

> Though to write much, in a little time, is no excuse for writing
> ill; yet Sir John Vanbrugh's pen is not to be a little admir'd for its
> spirit, ease, and readiness, in producing plays so fast, upon the neck
> of one another; for, notwithstanding this quick dispatch, there is a
> clear and lively simplicity in his wit, that neither wants the ornament
> of learning, nor has the least smell of the lamp in it. As the face of
> a fine woman, with only her locks loose about her, may be then in
> its greatest beauty; such are his productions, only adorn'd by nature.
> There is something so catching to the ear, so easy to the memory, in
> all he writ, that it has been observ'd by all the actors of my time, that
> the style of no author whatsoever gave their memory less trouble than
> that of Sir John Vanbrugh; which I myself, who have been charg'd
> with several of his strongest characters, can confirm by a pleasing
> experience. And indeed his wit and humour was so little laboured,
> that his most entertaining scenes seem'd to be no more than his

[13] *The Relapse*, edited by Curt A. Zimansky (Regents Restoration Drama
Series), 1970, p. xviii.

common conversation committed to paper. Here I confess my judgment at a loss, whether, in this, I give him more, or less, than his due praise? For may it not be more laudable to raise an estate (whether in wealth or fame) by pains, and honest industry, than to be born to it? Yet, if his scenes really were, as to me they always seem'd, delightful, are they not, thus, expeditiously written, the more surprising? Let the wit and merit of them, then, be weigh'd by wiser criticks than I pretend to be. But no wonder, while his conceptions were so full of life and humour, his muse should be sometimes too warm to wait the slow pace of judgment, or to endure the drudgery of forming a regular fable to them. Yet we see *The Relapse*, however imperfect, in the conduct, by the mere force of its agreeable wit, ran away with the hearts of its hearers; while *Love's Last Shift*, which (as Mr. Congreve justly said of it) had only in it a great many things that were *like* wit, that in reality were *not* wit; and what is still less pardonable (as I say of it myself) has a great deal of puerility and frothy stage-language in it, yet by the mere moral delight receiv'd from its fable, it has been, with the other, in a continued and equal possession of the stage for more than forty years.[14]

Something of Cibber's generosity of spirit is needed when we propose to judge Vanbrugh's dramatic language. Cibber, himself, was inclined to be something of a wit and a fop; that he should have delivered such a testimony to Vanbrugh's command of language might give us more pause in passing easy judgment on Vanbrugh's alleged easiness of disposition than the opinion of merely literary critics. If actors find it attractive to handle Vanbrugh's language, literary critics should be the more cautious in attacking it.

Such remarks apply to all those sections of Vanbrugh's text in *The Relapse* which have merited suspicion. In the opening scene of the play Loveless declares his affection for Amanda in the following terms:

> The largest boons that heaven thinks fit to grant,
> To things it has decreed shall crawl on earth,
> Are in the gift of women formed like you.
> Perhaps, when time shall be no more,
> When the aspiring soul shall take its flight,
> And drop this pond'rous lump of clay behind it,
> It may have appetites we know not of,
> And pleasures as refined as its desires—
> But till that day of knowledge shall instruct me,
> The utmost blessing that my thought can reach,
> (*Taking her in his arms*)
> Is folded in my arms, and rooted in my heart.
> AMANDA
> There let it grow for ever!   (I, i, 28–39)

[14] Colley Cibber, *An Apology for his Life* (Everyman edition, 1938), pp. 114–15.

Against this acceptable use of blank verse to convey an elevated experience Vanbrugh opposes the prose scene of II, i, in which Loveless and Amanda are in town. In reading this contrast might well be missed, but in performance the alteration of tone is inescapable, and Loveless's expression of devotion, because so over-stated, is retrospectively devalued. This is a skilful use of blank verse for inflation and deflation, and should prevent us from too quick a judgment of Vanbrugh's handling of language. Amanda's long speech at the beginning of V, iv reveals a similar complexity; her thoughts rise to blank verse when alone, stabilise themselves in initial confrontation with Worthy, and are then reduced to prose; this simulates, surely, some kind of reduction from fantasy to reality. Equally, Worthy's language, whether printed as verse or prose, should give the actor every opportunity to exploit the situation to the full. Worthy's final case, with us, rests upon his ability to convince us that his original attempt upon Amanda's virtue was uncharacteristic; to do so he needs every assistance that the language can muster, so that one pose can collapse convincingly into its opposite; perhaps Vanbrugh's ventures into blank verse, in this play, should be similarly viewed as indications of heroic posturing at the moment of imminent collapse.

As with language, so with character and scene, Vanbrugh usually improved what he borrowed. His Lord Foppington so pleased its creator that Cibber retained the peer in his own best play, *The Careless Husband*; the borrowed episode of Loveless's seduction of the compliant Berinthia, which critics relate to a scene in Crowne's *City Politiques* (II, i), is done with rather more panache. And when Vanbrugh parodied Cibber's final masque in celebration of Fame, Reason, Love, Honour, and Marriage with his own down-to-earth 'Dialogue between Cupid and Hymen' he brought far more dramatic point to bear upon this scene than is to be found in his model; for Vanbrugh's wedding guests sing the roistering chorus asserting the inevitability of change only to discover that this is just what lies in store for them when Young Fashion contrives the denouement.

The dialogue of Cupid and Hymen is a device for revealing the relationship between Vanbrugh's two plots: *The Provok'd Wife* and *A Journey to London* both contain admirable scenes of wooing and of marital disharmony; but *The Relapse* had already set Vanbrugh's distinctive pattern in dealing with both courtship and marriage with cynicism, some moral bravery, much social impudence, and sustained comic pace.

NOTE ON THE STAGE HISTORY

The Relapse has too full a stage history to recount in any detail. As Bonamy Dobrée observes, 'It held the stage successfully for over fifty years, being played nearly every one of them, sometimes at more than one theatre.'[15] After the mid-century, performances are less frequent, and when they do occur are likely to be of a play rather altered from the original. *The Relapse* was eventually adapted, for what the *Oxford Companion to the Theatre* calls 'a more prudish stage', first by John Lee, as *The Man of Quality* in 1773, and then by Sheridan as *A Trip to Scarborough* in 1777. This last adaptation, as Dobrée remarks, seems to have killed the original play for many years. Even when *The Relapse* was revived in its true form in 1846 at the Olympic Theatre it seems to have given way again to further adaptations. John Hollingshead opened the Gaiety Theatre in 1868, and contributed an adaptation of an adaptation with *The Man of Quality* in 1870 to a programme of productions which concentrated largely on the burlesque theatre during his spell as manager. Twenty years later Robert Buchanan's *Miss Tomboy* was performed at the Vaudeville Theatre in 1890.

Vanbrugh was surprisingly neglected during the first half of the present century, though provincial companies were more adventurous than London; amends were made in the most brilliant of post-war revivals of Restoration comedy, Anthony Quayle's production of *The Relapse* at the Phoenix Theatre in 1947 which gave the play a good run. It has been revived again, though less successfully, by the Royal Shakespeare Theatre Company in 1968. Meanwhile the adaptation of *The Relapse* as a musical entitled *Virtue in Danger*, by Paul Dehn and 'John Bernard', produced at the Mermaid Theatre in 1963, has become a genuine competitor with the original rather than a weak imitator. One of the strong advantages which this version has over previous adaptations is that it does not try to subvert the main plot by overplaying the secondary plot; Worthy and Berinthia come into their own with musical numbers which replace some of the hazards of their original dialogue. It seems an entirely natural con-

---

[15] *The Complete Works of Sir John Vanbrugh*, Vol. I, 6. Corrections and fresh information will be found in *The London Stage 1660–1800*, ed. by W. Van Lennep, E. L. Avery, A. H. Scouten, G. Winchester Stone Jr., and C. B. Hogan (Carbondale, Illinois, 1960–69); and there is a convenient summary of the stage history in C. A. Zimansky's edition, noted above, pp. xxi–xxiii.

clusion, drawn by men of the theatre rather than by literary scholars, that just as the proper evolution of heroic tragedy should be in the direction of opera, so the proper line of development for Vanbrugh's mixed heroics and humour should be in musical comedy.[16] This is the form to which *The Relapse* aspires, and which, with professional help, it attains.

[16] It is interesting to note that *Words for the Musick, in The Relapse: or, Vertue in Danger* (?1708), contains the texts of the song in Act IV, and of the 'Dialogue in the Last Act, Between Cupid and Hymen'. The minor textual differences do not warrant notice, but the publication suggests a continued public interest in the songs themselves more than a decade after their first performance.

NOTE ON THE TEXT

The only 'authority' for the text of *The Relapse* lies with the first quarto of 1697 (title-page date), which was followed by the quartos of 1698 and 1708. The first 'collected' edition of Vanbrugh's plays was made in 1719, but omitted *The Country House* and *A Journey to London*. The first of these plays was also omitted in the collected editions of 1730 and 1734; the first edition which might be said to be a collected edition is the two-volume octavo edition of 1735.

I have taken as my copy-text the Library of Congress copy of the 1697 quarto, which has been compared with the British Museum copies of this and the subsequent separately printed quartos, with the Dyson Collection copy of the 1719 edition, and with my own copies of the 1719 and 1735 editions. The text, though wretchedly printed, raises few real difficulties. Probably the compositor underestimated the length of the play, which is rather long by the standards of the day, and ran into difficulties in the later section of the play; understandably, too, he met trouble with Vanbrugh's loose verse. But I have not thought it sensible to record the many trivial typographical issues raised by careless printing, and by problems of punctuation—such as the inordinate use of the dash in company with regular marks of punctuation—and have confined my notation to a few matters which might mislead a reader. Modernisation presents few problems in the case of Vanbrugh, since his language is already modern, but I have regularised a few expletives (such as I'cod as ecod) and subdued a few exclamation marks in what is perhaps a rather over-emphatically printed first quarto. Act and scene divisions have been regularised.

ABBREVIATIONS

CE   Collected edition of 1719.
ed.   editor.
O.E.D. *Oxford English Dictionary*.
PMLA Publications of the Modern Language Association of America.
Q1   first quarto of 1697.
s.d.   stage direction.
s.p.   speech prefix.
1735   two-volume edition of 1735.

FURTHER READING

Stage

Allardyce Nicoll, *A History of English Drama, 1660–1900*, Vol. I (1923), and Vol. II (1925), and subsequent revised editions.

The London Stage 1660–1800, ed. by W. Van Lennep, E. L. Avery, A. H. Scouten, G. Winchester Stone Jr., and C. B. Hogan (Carbondale, Illinois, 1960–69).

J. Collier, *A Short View of the Immorality and Profaneness of the English Stage* (1698).

Sir John Vanbrugh, *A Short Vindication of 'The Relapse' and 'The Provok'd Wife', from Immorality and Prophaneness* (1698), reprinted in Dobrée and Webb, *The Complete Works of Sir John Vanbrugh* (1927), Vol. I, 193–215.

Editions

Bonamy Dobrée and Geoffrey Webb, *The Complete Works of Sir John Vanbrugh*, 4 vols. (1927), Vol. I.

Dougald MacMillan, and Howard M., Jones, *Plays of the Restoration and Eighteenth Century* (New York, 1931): also contains Cibber's *Love's Last Shift*.

George H. Nettleton, and Arthur E., Case, *British Dramatists from Dryden to Sheridan* (Boston, 1939).

C. A. Zimansky, *The Relapse* (Regents Renaissance Drama Series), 1970.

Criticism

William Hazlitt, *Lectures on the English Comic Writers* (1819).

John Palmer, *The Comedy of Manners* (1913).

Bonamy Dobrée, *Restoration Comedy* (1924).

J. W. Krutch, *Comedy and Conscience after the Restoration* (1924).

H. T. E. Perry, *The Comic Spirit in the Restoration Drama* (1925).

P. Mueschke and J. Fleischer, 'A Re-evaluation of Vanbrugh', *PMLA*, Vol. XLIX (1934).

J. Loftis, *Comedy and Society from Congreve to Fielding* (1959).

Restoration Theatre, ed. J. R. Brown and B. A. Harris, Stratford-upon-Avon Studies 6 (1965).

Restoration Drama: modern essays in criticism, ed. J. Loftis (1966).

B. A. Harris, *Sir John Vanbrugh* (Writers and their Work No. 197: 1967).

Peter Holland, *The Ornament of Action, Text and performance in restoration comedy* (Cambridge, 1979).

Hughes Derek, 'Vanbrugh and Cibber: Language, Place, and Social Order'. *The Relapse, Comparative Drama* Spring 21 (1) 1987, p.62-83. [Cf. "Cibber and Vanbrugh: Language, Place, and Social Order in *Love's Last Shift,"* *Comparative Drama* Winter 20(4) (1986/1987), 287–304]

McCormick, Frank, *Sir John Vanbrugh: The Playwright as Architect.* University Park: Pennsylvania State University Press, 1991.

——*Sir John Vanbrugh: A Reference Guide.* New York: Hall, 1992. [Bibliography of primary and secondary literature, 1694–1990]

Gill, James E., 'Character, Plot, and the Language of Love in *The Relapse:* A Reappraisal', *Restoration: Studies in English Literary Culture, 1660–1700* Fall 16(2) 1992, 110–25.

Braverman, Richard, *Plots and Counterplots. Sexual Politics and the Body Politic in English Literature, 1660–1730.* Cambridge: CUP, 1993.

Canfield, J. Douglas & Payne, Deborah C. (eds), *Cultural Readings of Restoration and Eighteenth-Century English Theater.* Athens & London: University of Georgia, 1995.

Comensoli, Viviana, *Household Business: Domestic Plays of Early Modern England,* Toronto, 1996.

Drougge, Helga, 'Anxiety in Vanbrugh's *The Relapse*', *Studies in English Literature*, 34 (3) 1994, 507-22.

THE
RELAPSE;

OR,

Virtue in Danger:

Being the Sequel of

The Fool in Fashion,

A

COMEDY.

ACTED AT

The *Theatre-Royal* in *Drury-lane* ;

Printed for *Samuel Briscoe* at the corner of *Charles-street* in *Russel-street* *Covent-Garden.* 1697.

Next week will be Publish'd Familiar Letters, the Second Volumn written by the Right Honourable John late Earl of *Rochester*, the Duke of *Buckingham* Sir *George Etheridge*, the Honourable *Henry Savill*, Esq; with other Letters, by a Person of Honour.

THE PREFACE

To go about to excuse half the defects this abortive brat is
come into the world with, would be to provoke the town with
a long useless preface, when 'tis, I doubt, sufficiently soured
already by a tedious play.

I do therefore (with all the humility of a repenting sinner) con-   5
fess, it wants everything—but length: and in that, I hope, the
severest critic will be pleased to acknowledge I have not been
wanting. But my modesty will sure atone for everything, when
the world shall know it is so great, I am even to this day in-
sensible of those two shining graces in the play (which some   10
part of the town is pleased to compliment me with)—blasphemy and bawdy.

For my part, I cannot find 'em out. If there were any obscene
expressions upon the stage, here they are in the print; for I
have dealt fairly, I have not sunk a syllable that could (though   15
by racking of mysteries) be ranged under that head; and yet I
believe with a steady faith, there is not one woman of a real
reputation in town, but when she has read it impartially over
in her closet, will find it so innocent, she'll think it no affront to
her prayer book to lay it upon the same shelf. So to them (with   20
all manner of deference) I entirely refer my cause; and I'm
confident they'll justify me against those pretenders to good
manners, who, at the same time, have so little respect for the
ladies they would extract a bawdy jest from an ejaculation, to
put 'em out of countenance. But I expect to have these well-   25
bred persons always my enemies, since I'm sure I shall never
write anything lewd enough to make 'em my friends.

As for the saints (your thorough-paced ones, I mean, with
screwed faces and wry mouths) I despair of them, for they are
friends to nobody. They love nothing but their altars and   30
themselves. They have too much zeal to have any charity: they
make debauches in piety, as sinners do in wine; and are as
quarrelsome in their religion as other people are in their drink;
so I hope nobody will mind what they say. But if any man
(with flat plod shoes, a little band, greasy hair, and a dirty face,   35

12 Attacks upon stage morals had already been made by Sir Richard
   Blackmore and James Wright, anticipating Collier.
13 *were* (CE) was (Q1)

3

2

who is wiser than I, at the expense of being forty years older)
happens to be offended at a story of a cock and a bull, and a
priest and a bulldog, I beg his pardon with all my heart, which
I hope I shall obtain by eating my words and making this public
recantation. I do therefore, for his satisfaction, acknowledge I   40
lied when I said they never quit their hold; for in that little
time I have lived in the world, I thank God I have seen 'em
forced to it more than once; but next time I'll speak with
more caution and truth, and only say, they have very good
teeth.   45

If I have offended any honest gentlemen of the town, whose
friendship or good word is worth the having, I am very sorry for
it; I hope they'll correct me as gently as they can, when they
consider I have had no other design, in running a very great
risk, than to divert (if possible) some part of their spleen, in   50
spite of their wives and their taxes.

One word more about the bawdy, and I have done. I own the
first night this thing was acted some indecencies had like to
have happened, but 'twas not my fault.

The fine gentleman of the play, drinking his mistress's   55
health in Nantes brandy, from six in the morning to the time
he waddled on upon the stage in the evening, had toasted himself up to such a pitch of vigour I confess I once gave Amanda
for gone, and I am since (with all due respect to Mrs Rogers)
very sorry she scaped; for I am confident a certain lady (let no   60
one take it to herself that's handsome) who highly blames the
play, for the barrenness of the conclusion, would then have
allowed it a very natural close.

55 *fine gentleman* George Powell, who played Worthy, drank.

FIRST PROLOGUE
Spoken by Miss Cross

Ladies, this play in too much haste was writ,
To be o'ercharged with either plot or wit;
'Twas got, conceived, and born in six weeks' space,
And wit, you know, 's as slow in growth as grace.
Sure it can ne'er be ripened to your taste;   5
I doubt 'twill prove, our author bred too fast:
For mark 'em well, who with the Muses marry,
They rarely do conceive, but they miscarry.
'Tis the hard fate of those wh' are big with rhyme,
Still to be brought to bed before their time.   10
Of our late poets Nature few has made;
The greatest part—are only so by trade.
Still want of something brings the scribbling fit;
For want of money some of 'em have writ,
And others do't, you see—for want of wit.   15
Honour, they fancy, summons 'em to write,
So out they lug in resty Nature's spite,
As some of you spruce beaux do—when you fight.
Yet let the ebb of wit be ne'er so low,
Some glimpse of it a man may hope to show,   20
Upon a theme so ample—as a beau.
So, howsoe'er true courage may decay,
Perhaps there's not one smock-face here today
But's bold as Caesar—to attack a play;
Nay, what's yet more, with an undaunted face,   25
To do the thing with more heroic grace;
'Tis six to four y'attack the strongest place.
You are such Hotspurs in this kind of venture,
Where there's no breach, just there you needs must enter.
But be advised—   30
E'en give the hero and the critic o'er,
For Nature sent you on another score—
She formed her beau, for nothing but her whore.

s.p. *Miss Cross* The 'Mrs' of the cast list probably means 'Mistress'.
     Dobrée notes a line in Farquhar's *Love and a Bottle* (1699):
       O Collier! Collier! thou'st frighted away Miss Cross.
17 *resty* impatient   23 *smock-face* effeminate in appearance

5

THE PROLOGUE ON THE THIRD DAY
Spoken by Mrs Verbruggen

Apologies for plays, experience shows,
Are things almost as useless—as the beaux.
Whate'er we say (like them) we neither move
Your friendship, pity, anger, nor your love.
'Tis interest turns the globe: let us but find   5
The way to please you, and you'll soon be kind:
But to expect you'd for our sakes approve,
Is just as though you for their sakes should love;
And that, we do confess, we think a task,
Which (though they may impose) we never ought to ask.   10

This is an age where all things we improve,
But, most of all, the art of making love.
In former days, women were only won
By merit, truth, and constant service done;
But lovers now are much more expert grown;   15
They seldom wait t'approach by tedious form;
They're for dispatch, for taking you by storm:
Quick are their sieges, furious are their fires,
Fierce their attacks, and boundless their desires.
Before the play's half ended, I'll engage   20
To show you beaux come crowding on the stage,
Who with so little pains have always sped,
They'll undertake to look a lady dead.
How I have shook, and trembling stood with awe,
When here, behind the scenes, I've seen 'em draw   25
—A comb; that dead-doing weapon to the heart,
And turn each powdered hair into a dart.
When I have seen 'em sally on the stage,
Dressed to the war, and ready to engage,
I've mourned your destiny—yet more their fate,   30
To think, that after victories so great,
It should so often prove their hard mishap
To sneak into a lane—and get a clap.
But, hush! they're here already; I'll retire,
And leave 'em to you ladies to admire.   35
They'll show you twenty thousand airs and graces,

7

They'll entertain you with their soft grimaces,
Their snuff-box, awkward bows—and ugly faces.
In short, they're after all so much your friends,
That lest the play should fail the author's ends,   40
They have resolved to make you some amends.
Between each act (performed by nicest rules)
They'll treat you—with an interlude of fools:
Of which, that you may have the deeper sense,
The entertainment's—at their own expense.   45

DRAMATIS PERSONAE

Men

SIR NOVELTY FASHION, *newly created* LORD FOPPINGTON	*Mr Cibber*
YOUNG FASHION, *his brother*	*Mrs Kent*
LOVELESS, *husband to Amanda*	*Mr Verbruggen*
WORTHY, *a gentleman of the town*	*Mr Powell* 5
SIR TUNBELLY CLUMSEY, *a country gentleman*	*Mr Bullock*
SIR JOHN FRIENDLY, *his neighbour*	*Mr Mills*
COUPLER, *a matchmaker*	*Mr Johnson*
BULL, *chaplain to Sir Tunbelly*	*Mr Simson*
SYRINGE, *a surgeon*	*Mr Haynes* 10
LORY, *servant to Young Fashion*	*Mr Dogget*
SHOEMAKER, TAILOR, PERIWIG-MAKER, *etc.*	

Women

AMANDA, *wife to Loveless*	*Mrs Rogers*
BERINTHIA, *her cousin, a young widow*	*Mrs Verbruggen*
MISS HOYDEN, *a great Fortune, daughter to*	15
Sir Tunbelly	*Mrs Cross*
NURSE, *her governant*	*Mrs Powell*

10 SYRINGE Serringe (Q1)
14 BERINTHIA Berrinthia (Q1)
17 *governant* Gouvernante (Q1)

9

THE RELAPSE, or VIRTUE IN DANGER

Act I, Scene i

Enter LOVELESS *reading*

LOVELESS

How true is that philosophy which says
Our heaven is seated in our minds!
Through all the roving pleasures of my youth,
(Where nights and days seemed all consumed in joy,
Where the false face of luxury   5
Displayed such charms,
As might have shaken the most holy hermit,
And made him totter at his altar),
I never knew one moment's peace like this.
Here, in this little soft retreat,   10
My thoughts unbent from all the cares of life,
Content with fortune,
Eased from the grating duties of dependence,
From envy free, ambition under foot,
The raging flame of wild destructive lust   15
Reduced to a warm pleasing fire of lawful love,
My life glides on, and all is well within.

Enter AMANDA

LOVELESS (*Meeting her kindly*)
How does the happy cause of my content,
My dear Amanda?
You find me musing on my happy state,   20
And full of grateful thoughts to heaven, and you.
AMANDA
Those grateful offerings heaven can't receive
With more delight than I do:
Would I could share with it as well

---

1 s.d. Q1 lacks many specific scene locations. This is clearly a
   room in Loveless's country home.
s.p. LOVELESS Lovelace (Q1) a frequent misspelling, regularised
   hereafter without further note

11

The dispensations of its bliss,   25
That I might search its choicest favours out,
And shower'em on your head for ever!
LOVELESS
The largest boons that heaven thinks fit to grant,
To things it has decreed shall crawl on earth
Are in the gift of women formed like you.   30
Perhaps, when time shall be no more,
When the aspiring soul shall take its flight,
And drop this pond'rous lump of clay behind it,
It may have appetites we know not of,
And pleasures as refined as its desires—   35
But till that day of knowledge shall instruct me,
The utmost blessing that my thought can reach,
(*Taking her in his arms*)
Is folded in my arms, and rooted in my heart.
AMANDA
There let it grow for ever!
LOVELESS
Well said, Amanda—let it be for ever—   40
Would heaven grant that—
AMANDA
                          'Twere all the heaven I'd ask.
But we are clad in black mortality,
And the dark curtain of eternal night
At last must drop between us.
LOVELESS
                          It must;
That mournful separation we must see.   45
A bitter pill it is to all; but doubles its ungrateful taste
When lovers are to swallow it.
AMANDA
Perhaps that pain may only be my lot,
You possibly may be exempted from it,
Men find out softer ways to quench their fires.   50
LOVELESS
Can you then doubt my constancy, Amanda?
You'll find 'tis built upon a steady basis—
The rock of reason now supports my love,
On which it stands so fixed,
The rudest hurricane of wild desire   55

40–44 printed as prose (Q1). Such minor adjustments of lineation
are not recorded hereafter.

Would, like the breath of a soft slumbering babe,
Pass by, and never shake it.

AMANDA

Yet still 'tis safer to avoid the storm;
The strongest vessels, if they put to sea,
May possibly be lost.   60
Would I could keep you here, in this calm port, for ever!
Forgive the weakness of a woman;
I am uneasy at your going to stay so long in town;
I know its false insinuating pleasures;
I know the force of its delusions;   65
I know the strength of its attacks;
I know the weak defence of nature;
I know you are a man—and I—a wife.

LOVELESS

You know then all that needs to give you rest,
For wife's the strongest claim that you can urge.   70
When you would plead your title to my heart,
On this you may depend. Therefore be calm,
Banish your fears, for they are traitors to your peace:
Beware of 'em,
They are insinuating busy things   75
That gossip to and fro,
And do a world of mischief where they come.
But you shall soon be mistress of 'em all;
I'll aid you with such arms for their destruction,
They never shall erect their heads again.   80
You know the business is indispensable
That obliges me to go to London;
And you have no reason, that I know of,
To believe I'm glad of the occasion.
For my honest conscience is my witness,   85
I have found a due succession of such charms
In my retirement here with you,
I have never thrown one roving thought that way;
But since, against my will, I'm dragged once more
To that uneasy theatre of noise,   90
I am resolved to make such use on't
As shall convince you 'tis an old cast mistress,
Who has been so lavish of her favours,
She's now grown bankrupt of her charms,
And has not one allurement left to move me.   95

92 *cast* cast off

AMANDA

    Her bow, I do believe, is grown so weak,
    Her arrows (at this distance) cannot hurt you;
    But in approaching 'em, you give 'em strength.
    The dart that has not far to fly, will put
    The best of armour to a dangerous trial.   100

LOVELESS

    That trial past, and y'are at ease for ever;
    When you have seen the helmet proved,
    You'll apprehend no more for him that wears it.
    Therefore to put a lasting period to your fears,
    I am resolved, this once, to launch into temptation;   105
    I'll give you an essay of all my virtues;
    My former boon companions of the bottle
    Shall fairly try what charms are left in wine:
    I'll take my place amongst 'em,
    They shall hem me in,   110
    Sing praises to their god, and drink his glory;
    Turn wild enthusiasts for his sake,
    And beasts to do him honour:
    Whilst I, a stubborn atheist,
    Sullenly look on,   115
    Without one reverend glass to his divinity.
    That for my temperance,
    Then for my constancy—

AMANDA   Ay, there take heed.

LOVELESS   Indeed the danger's small.

AMANDA   And yet my fears are great

LOVELESS   Why are you so timorous?

AMANDA   Because you are so bold.   120

LOVELESS

    My courage should disperse your apprehensions.

AMANDA

    My apprehensions should alarm your courage.

LOVELESS

    Fie, fie, Amanda! It is not kind thus to distrust me.

AMANDA

    And yet my fears are founded on my love.

LOVELESS

    Your love then is not founded as it ought;   125
    For if you can believe 'tis possible
    I should again relapse to my past follies,
    I must appear to you a thing
    Of such an undigested composition,

That but to think of me with inclination,　　　　130
Would be a weakness in your taste,
Your virtue scarce could answer.

AMANDA

'Twould be a weakness in my tongue
My prudence could not answer,
If I should press you farther with my fears;　　　135
I'll therefore trouble you no longer with 'em.

LOVELESS

Nor shall they trouble you much longer.
A little time shall show you they were groundless:
This winter shall be the fiery trial of my virtue,
Which, when it once has passed,　　　　140
You'll be convinced 'twas of no false allay,
There all your cares will end.

AMANDA　　　　　　　　　Pray heaven they may.
　　　　　　　　　　　　　(*Exeunt, hand in hand*)

Act I, Scene ii

Whitehall

Enter YOUNG FASHION, LORY, *and* WATERMAN

FASHION

Come, pay the waterman, and take the portmantle.

LORY

Faith, sir, I think the waterman had as good take the portmantle, and pay himself.

FASHION

Why, sure there's something left in 't!

LORY

But a solitary old waistcoat, upon honour, sir.　　　5

FASHION

Why, what's become of the blue coat, sirrah?

LORY

Sir, 'twas eaten at Gravesend; the reckoning came to thirty
shillings, and your privy purse was worth but two half-
crowns.

FASHION

'Tis very well.　　　　10

WATERMAN

Pray, master, will you please to dispatch me?

---

1 *portmantle* travelling-bag

FASHION

Ay, here, a —canst thou change me a guinea?

LORY (*Aside*)

Good.

WATERMAN

Change a guinea, master! Ha! ha! your honour's pleased to
compliment.   15

FASHION

Egad, I don't know how I shall pay thee then, for I have
nothing but gold about me.

LORY (*Aside*)

Hum, hum.

FASHION

What dost thou expect, friend?

WATERMAN

Why, master, so far against wind and tide is richly worth   20
half a piece.

FASHION

Why, faith, I think thou art a good conscionable fellow.
Egad, I begin to have so good an opinion of thy honesty,
I care not if I leave my portmantle with thee, till I send thee
thy money.   25

WATERMAN

Ha! God bless your honour; I should be as willing to trust
you master, but that you are, as a man may say, a stranger
to me, and these are nimble times; there are a great many
sharpers stirring. (*Taking up the portmantle*) Well, master,
when your worship sends the money, your portmantle shall   30
be forthcoming; my name's Tug; my wife keeps a brandy-
shop in Drab-Alley, at Wapping.

FASHION

Very well; I'll send for't tomorrow.

(*Exit* WATERMAN)

LORY

So. Now, sir, I hope you'll own yourself a happy man, you
have outlived all your cares.   35

FASHION

How so, sir?

LORY

Why, you have nothing left to take care of.

21 *half a piece* roughly, half a guinea
32 *Drab-Alley, at Wapping* Vanbrugh seems to have invented a
   street to accommodate some customary inhabitants of this
   Thames-side locality.

FASHION
Yes, sirrah, I have myself and you to take care of still.

LORY
Sir, if you could but prevail with somebody else to do that for
you, I fancy we might both fare the better for't.   40

FASHION
Why, if thou canst tell me where to apply myself, I have at
present so little money and so much humility about me, I
don't know but I may follow a fool's advice.

LORY
Why then, sir, your fool advises you to lay aside all animosity,
and apply to Sir Novelty, your elder brother.   45

FASHION
Damn my elder brother!

LORY
With all my heart; but get him to redeem your annuity,
however.

FASHION
My annuity! 'Sdeath, he's such a dog, he would not give his
powder-puff to redeem my soul.   50

LORY
Look you, sir, you must wheedle him, or you must starve.

FASHION
Look you, sir, I will neither wheedle him, nor starve.

LORY
Why, what will you do then?

FASHION
I'll go into the army.

LORY
You can't take the oaths; you are a Jacobite.   55

FASHION
Thou may'st as well say I can't take orders because I'm an
atheist.

LORY
Sir, I ask your pardon; I find I did not know the strength of
your conscience so well as I did the weakness of your purse.

FASHION
Methinks, sir, a person of your experience should have   60
known that the strength of the conscience proceeds from the
weakness of the purse.

50 *powder-puff* for the wig, not the face
55 *Jacobite* a supporter of James II

LORY

Sir, I am very glad to find you have a conscience able to take
care of us, let it proceed from what it will; but I desire you'll
please to consider, that the army alone will be but a scant   65
maintenance for a person of your generosity (at least as rents
now are paid). I shall see you stand in damnable need of
some auxiliary guineas for your *menus plaisirs*; I will therefore turn fool once more for your service, and advise you to
go directly to your brother.   70

FASHION

Art thou then so impregnable a blockhead, to believe he'll
help me with a farthing?

LORY

Not if you treat him *de haut en bas*, as you use to do.

FASHION

Why, how wouldst have me treat him?

LORY

Like a trout—tickle him.   75

FASHION

I can't flatter.

LORY

Can you starve?

FASHION

Yes.

LORY

I can't. Good-bye t'ye, sir—   (*Going*)

FASHION

Stay; thou wilt distract me! What wouldst thou have me say   80
to him?

LORY

Say nothing to him, apply yourself to his favourites, speak
to his periwig, his cravat, his feather, his snuff-box, and when
you are well with them—desire him to lend you a thousand
pounds. I'll engage you prosper.   85

FASHION

'Sdeath and furies! Why was that coxcomb thrust into the
world before me? O Fortune! Fortune!—thou art a bitch, by
Gad.   (*Exeunt*)

66 *rents* pay, or salary
68 *your menus* you *menu* (Q1): *menus plaisirs* trifling pleasures

Act I, Scene iii

A dressing room
Enter LORD FOPPINGTON *in his night-gown*

LORD FOPPINGTON
  Page!

Enter PAGE

PAGE
  Sir.
LORD FOPPINGTON
  Sir! Pray, sir, do me the favour to teach your tongue the
  title the king has thought fit to honour me with.
PAGE
  I ask your lordship's pardon, my lord.   5
LORD FOPPINGTON
  Oh, you can pronounce the word then? I thought it would
  have choked you. D'ye hear?
PAGE
  My lord!
LORD FOPPINGTON
  Call La Vérole: I would dress. (*Exit* PAGE. *Solus*)—Well, 'tis
  an unspeakable pleasure to be a man of quality, strike me   10
  dumb!—My lord.—Your lordship—My Lord Foppington
  —*Ah! c'est quelque chose de beau, que le diable m'emporte!*—
  Why, the ladies were ready to puke at me whilst I had
  nothing but Sir Navelty to recommend me to 'em.—Sure,
  whilst I was but a knight, I was a very nauseous fellow.—   15
  Well, 'tis ten thousand pawnd well given, stap my vitals!—

Enter LA VÉROLE

LA VÉROLE
  Me lord, de shoemaker, de tailor, de hosier, de sempstress,
  de barber, be all ready, if your lordship please to be dress.
LORD FOPPINGTON
  'Tis well, admit 'em.
LA VÉROLE
  Hey, *messieurs, entrez.*   20

Enter TAILOR *&c.*

___

  9 *Vérole* the name means syphilis
  18 *to be dress* (Q1) to dress (CE)

LORD FOPPINGTON

So, gentlemen, I hope you have all taken pains to show yourselves masters in your professions.

TAILOR

I think I may presume to say, sir—

LA VÉROLE

My lord—you clawn, you.

TAILOR

Why, is he made a lord? My lord, I ask your lordship's   25
pardon, my lord; I hope, my lord, your lordship will please to own I have brought your lordship as accomplished a suit of clothes as ever peer of England trod the stage in, my lord. Will your lordship please to try 'em now?

LORD FOPPINGTON

Ay; but let my people dispose the glasses so, that I may see   30
myself before and behind, for I love to see myself all raund.

Whilst he puts on his clothes, enter
YOUNG FASHION *and* LORY

FASHION

Heyday, what the devil have we here? Sure my gentleman's grown a favourite at court, he has got so many people at his levee.

LORY

Sir, these people come in order to make him a favourite at   35
court, they are to establish him with the ladies.

FASHION

Good God! to what an ebb of taste are women fallen, that it should be in the power of a laced coat to recommend a gallant to 'em!

LORY

Sir, tailors and periwig-makers are now become the bawds   40
of the nation; 'tis they debauch all the women.

FASHION

Thou sayst true; for there's that fop now has not by nature wherewithal to move a cook-maid, and by that time these fellows have done with him, egad he shall melt down a countess!—But now for my reception; I'll engage it shall be   45
as cold a one as a courtier's to his friend who comes to put him in mind of his promise.

LORD FOPPINGTON (*To his* TAILOR)

Death and eternal tartures! Sir, I say the packet's too high by a foot.

28 *trod* (CE) trode (Q1) perhaps a pronunciation clue

TAILOR

My lord, if it had been an inch lower, it would not have held   50
your lordship's pocket-handkerchief.

LORD FOPPINGTON

Rat my pocket-handkerchief! have not I a page to carry it?
You may make him a packet up to his chin a purpose for it;
but I will not have mine come so near my face.

TAILOR

'Tis not for me to dispute your lordship's fancy.   55

FASHION (*To* LORY)

His lordship! Lory, did you observe that?

LORY

Yes, sir; I always thought 'twould end there. Now, I hope,
you'll have a little more respect for him.

FASHION

Respect!—Damn him for a coxcomb! Now has he ruined
his estate to buy a title, that he may be a fool of the first   60
rate. But let's accost him. (*To* LORD FOPPINGTON) Brother,
I'm your humble servant.

LORD FOPPINGTON

O Lard, Tam! I did not expect you in England. Brother, I am
glad to see you.—(*Turning to his* TAILOR) Look you, sir; I
shall never be reconciled to this nauseous packet; therefore   65
pray get me another suit with all manner of expedition, for
this is my eternal aversion.—Mrs Calico, are not you of my
mind?

SEMPSTRESS

Oh, directly, my lord! it can never be too low.

LORD FOPPINGTON

You are positively in the right on't, for the packet becomes   70
no part of the body but the knee.   (*Exit* TAILOR)

SEMPSTRESS

I hope your lordship is pleased with your Steenkirk.

LORD FOPPINGTON

In love with it, stap my vitals!—Bring your bill, you shall
be paid tomorrow.

SEMPSTRESS

I humbly thank your honour.   (*Exit* SEMPSTRESS)   75

LORD FOPPINGTON

Hark thee, shoemaker, these shoes an't ugly, but they don't
fit me.

72 *Steenkirk Stinkirk* (Q1) a loose cravat, adopted fashionably from
    the unready neckwear of the French cavalry at the battle of
    Steinkirk (1692)

SHOEMAKER

My lord, my thinks they fit you very well.

LORD FOPPINGTON

They hurt me just below the instep.

SHOEMAKER (*Feeling his foot*)

My lord, they don't hurt you there.   80

LORD FOPPINGTON

I tell thee they pinch me execrably.

SHOEMAKER

My lord, if they pinch you, I'll be bound to be hanged,
that's all.

LORD FOPPINGTON

Why, wilt thou undertake to persuade me I cannot feel?

SHOEMAKER

Your lordship may please to feel what you think fit; but that   85
shoe does not hurt you; I think I understand my trade.

LORD FOPPINGTON

Now by all that's great and powerful, thou art an incom-
prehensible coxcomb! But thou makest good shoes and so
I'll bear with thee.

SHOEMAKER

My lord, I have worked for half the people of quality in   90
town these twenty years; and 'twere very hard I should not
know when a shoe hurts, and when it don't.

LORD FOPPINGTON

Well, prithee be gone about thy business. (*Exit* SHOEMAKER)
(*To the* HOSIER) Mr Mendlegs, a word with you: the calves of
these stockings are thickened a little too much. They make   95
my legs look like a chairman's.

MENDLEGS

My lord, my thinks they look mighty well.

LORD FOPPINGTON

Ay, but you are not so good a judge of these things as I am,
I have studied 'em all my life; therefore pray let the next
be the thickness of a crawn-piece less—(*Aside*) If the town   100
takes notice my legs are fallen away, 'twill be attributed to
the violence of some new intrigue.   (*Exit* MENDLEGS)
(*To the* PERIWIG-MAKER) Come, Mr Foretop, let me see what
you have done, and then the fatigue of the marning will be
over.   105

FORETOP

My lord, I have done what I defy any prince in Europe t'

96 *chairman's* implying the thickness of a sedan-chair carrier's legs

outdo; I have made you a periwig so long, and so full of hair, it will serve for hat and cloak in all weathers.

LORD FOPPINGTON

Then thou hast made me thy friend to eternity. Come, comb it out.   110

FASHION (*Aside to* LORY)

Well, Lory, what dost think on't? A very friendly reception from a brother after three years' absence!

LORY

Why, sir, it's your own fault; we seldom care for those that don't love what we love: if you would creep into his heart, you must enter into his pleasures. Here have you   115 stood ever since you came in, and have not commanded any one thing that belongs to him.

FASHION

Nor never shall, whilst they belong to a coxcomb.

LORY

Then, sir, you must be content to pick a hungry bone.

FASHION

No, sir, I'll crack it, and get to the marrow before I have   120 done.

LORD FOPPINGTON

Gad's curse, Mr Foretop! you don't intend to put this upon me for a full periwig?

FORETOP

Not a full one, my lord! I don't know what your lordship may please to call a full one, but I have crammed twenty   125 ounces of hair into it.

LORD FOPPINGTON

What it may be by weight, sir, I shall not dispute; but by tale, there are not nine hairs of a side.

FORETOP

O Lord! O Lord! O Lord! Why, as Gad shall judge me, your honour's side-face is reduced to the tip of your nose!   130

LORD FOPPINGTON

My side-face may be in eclipse for aught I know; but I'm sure my full-face is like the full-moon.

FORETOP

Heavens bless my eye-sight—(*Rubbing his eyes*) Sure I look

---

107 Zimansky refers to a note in Pope's *Dunciad* (I.167), to the effect that Lord Foppington's periwig was carried on stage in a sedan-chair: the incident is associated with *Love's Last Shift*, but no doubt became traditional business.

128 *by tale* tally, counting by numbers

through the wrong-end of the perspective; for by my faith,
an't please your honour, the broadest place I see in your face   135
does not seem to me to be two inches diameter.

LORD FOPPINGTON

If it did, it would be just two inches too broad; far a periwig
to a man should be like a mask to a woman, nothing should
be seen but his eyes.

FORETOP

My lord, I have done; if you please to have more hair in   140
your wig, I'll put it in.

LORD FOPPINGTON

Pasitively, yes.

FORETOP

Shall I take it back now, my lord?

LORD FOPPINGTON

No: I'll wear it today, though it show such a manstrous pair
of cheeks, stap my vitals, I shall be taken for a trumpeter.   145

(*Exit* FORETOP)

FASHION

Now your people of business are gone, brother, I hope I may
obtain a quarter of an hour's audience of you.

LORD FOPPINGTON

Faith, Tam, I must beg you'll excuse me at this time, for I
must away to the House of Lards immediately; my Lady
Teaser's case is to come on today, and I would not be   150
absent for the salvation of mankind—Hey, page!

[*Enter* PAGE]

Is the coach at the door?

PAGE

Yes, my lord.

LORD FOPPINGTON

You'll excuse me, brother.   (*Going*)

FASHION

Shall you be back at dinner?   155

LORD FOPPINGTON

As Gad shall jidge me, I can't tell; for 'tis passible I may
dine with some of aur House at Lacket's.

FASHION

Shall I meet you there? For I must needs talk with you.

134 *perspective* telescope
157 *Lacket's* Locket's, a famous ordinary, or tavern, near Charing
     Cross

LORD FOPPINGTON

That I'm afraid mayn't be so praper; far the lards I commonly eat with are people of a nice conversation; and you   160
know, Tam, your education has been a little at large: but,
if you'll stay here, you'll find a family dinner.—[*To* PAGE]
Hey, fellow! What is there for dinner? There's beef: I
suppose my brother will eat beef. Dear Tam, I'm glad to
see thee in England, stap my vitals! (*Exit with his equipage*) 165

FASHION

Hell and furies! is this to be borne?

LORY

Faith, sir, I could almost have given him a knock o' th' pate
myself.

FASHION

'Tis enough; I will now show thee the excess of my passion
by being very calm. Come, Lory, lay your loggerhead to   170
mine, and in cool blood let us contrive his destruction.

LORY

Here comes a head, sir, would contrive it better than us
both, if he would but join in the confederacy.

Enter COUPLER

FASHION

By this light, old Coupler alive still!—Why, how now,
match-maker, art thou here still to plague the world with   175
matrimony? You old bawd, how have you the impudence to
be hobbling out of your grave twenty years after you are
rotten?

COUPLER

When you begin to rot, sirrah, you'll go off like a pippin;
one winter will send you to the devil. What mischief brings   180
you home again? Ha! you young lascivious rogue, you. Let
me put my hand in your bosom, sirrah.

FASHION

Stand off, old Sodom!

COUPLER

Nay, prithee now, don't be so coy.

FASHION

Keep your hands to yourself, you old dog you, or I'll wring   185
your nose off.

COUPLER

Hast thou then been a year in Italy, and brought home a
fool at last? By my conscience, the young fellows of this
age profit no more by their going abroad than they do by

their going to church. Sirrah, sirrah, if you are not hanged be-   190
fore you come to my years, you'll know a cock from a hen. But,
come, I'm still a friend to thy person, though I have a contempt of thy understanding; and therefore I would willingly
know thy condition, that I may see whether thou stand'st in
need of my assistance: for widows swarm, my boy, the   195
town's infected with 'em.

FASHION

I stand in need of anybody's assistance that will help me to
cut my elder brother's throat, without the risk of being
hanged for him.

COUPLER

Egad, sirrah, I could help thee to do him almost as good a   200
turn, without the danger of being burned in the hand for't.

FASHION

Sayest thou so, old Satan? Show me but that, and my soul is
thine.

COUPLER

Pox o'thy soul! give me thy warm body, sirrah; I shall have
a substantial title to't when I tell thee my project.   205

FASHION

Out with it then, dear dad, and take possession as soon as
thou wilt.

COUPLER

Sayest thou so, my Hephestion? Why, then, thus lies the
scene.—But hold; who's that? if we are heard we are undone.

FASHION

What, have you forgot Lory?   210

COUPLER

Who? Trusty Lory, is it thee?

LORY

At your service, sir.

COUPLER

Give me thy hand, old boy. Egad, I did not know thee
again; but I remember thy honesty, though I did not thy
face; I think thou hadst like to have been hanged once or   215
twice for thy master.

LORY

Sir, I was very near once having that honour.

201 *burned in the hand* the punishment for thieves
208 *Hephestion* Alexander's favourite: Nathaniel Lee's *The Rival
Queens, or, the death of Alexander the Great* (1677) was a famous
tragedy of the era.
210 What have you forgot, Lory? (Q1)

COUPLER

Well, live and hope; don't be discouraged; eat with him, and
drink with him, and do what he bids thee, and it may be
thy reward at last, as well as another's.—(*To* YOUNG   220
FASHION) Well, sir, you must know I have done you the
kindness to make up a match for your brother.

FASHION

Sir, I am very much beholding to you, truly.

COUPLER

You may be, sirrah, before the wedding-day yet. The lady
is a great heiress; fifteen hundred pound a year, and a great   225
bag of money; the match is concluded, the writings are
drawn, and the pipkin's to be cracked in a fortnight. Now
you must know, stripling (with respect to your mother),
your brother's the son of a whore.

FASHION

Good!   230

COUPLER

He has given me a bond of a thousand pounds for helping
him to this fortune, and has promised me as much more in
ready money upon the day of marriage, which, I understand by a friend, he ne'er designs to pay me. If therefore
you will be a generous young dog, and secure me five   235
thousand pounds, I'll be a covetous old rogue, and help you
to the lady.

FASHION

Egad, if thou canst bring this about, I'll have thy statue cast
in brass. But don't you dote, you old pander you, when you
talk at this rate?   240

COUPLER

That your youthful parts shall judge of. This plump
partridge, that I tell you of, lives in the country, fifty miles
off, with her honoured parents, in a lonely old house which
nobody comes near; she never goes abroad, nor sees company at home. To prevent all misfortunes, she has her   245
breeding within doors; the parson of the parish teaches
her to play upon the bass-viol, the clerk to sing, her nurse
to dress, and her father to dance. In short, nobody can give
you admittance there but I; nor can I do it any other way
than by making you pass for your brother.   250

227 *the pipkin's to be cracked* the vessel's to be broached, an obvious
   reference to Miss Hoyden
242 *partridge* (CE) patridge (Q1)

FASHION

And how the devil wilt thou do that?

COUPLER

Without the devil's aid, I warrant thee. Thy brother's face not one of the family ever saw; the whole business has been managed by me, and all the letters go through my hands. The last that was writ to Sir Tunbelly Clumsey (for that's   255 the old gentleman's name), was to tell him, his lordship would be down in a fortnight to consummate. Now, you shall go away immediately, pretend you writ that letter only to have the romantic pleasure of surprising your mistress; fall desperately in love as soon as you see her; make that   260 your plea for marrying her immediately, and, when the fatigue of the wedding-night's over, you shall send me a swinging purse of gold, you dog you.

FASHION

Egad, old dad, I'll put my hand in thy bosom now.

COUPLER

Ah, you young hot lusty thief, let me muzzle you!—(*Kissing*)   265 Sirrah, let me muzzle you.

FASHION (*Aside*)

P'sha, the old lecher!

COUPLER

Well; I'll warrant thou hast not a farthing of money in thy pocket now; no, one may see it in thy face.

FASHION

Not a souse, by Jupiter!   270

COUPLER

Must I advance then? Well, sirrah, be at my lodgings in half an hour, and I'll see what may be done; we'll sign, and seal, and eat a pullet, and when I have given thee some farther instructions, thou shalt hoist sail and be gone. (*Kissing*) T'other buss, and so adieu.   275

FASHION

Um! P'sha!

COUPLER

Ah, you young warm dog you, what a delicious night will the bride have on't.   (*Exit* COUPLER)

FASHION

So, Lory; Providence, thou seest at last, takes care of men of merit; we are in a fair way to be great people.   280

257 *fortnight* (CE) forthnight (Q1)
270 *souse* sou

LORY

Ay, sir, if the devil don't step between the cup and the lip,
as he uses to do.

FASHION

Why, faith, he has played me many a damned trick to spoil
my fortune, and egad I'm almost afraid he's at work about
it again now; but if I should tell thee how, thou'dst wonder   285
at me.

LORY

Indeed, sir, I should not.

FASHION

How dost know?

LORY

Because, sir, I have wondered at you so often, I can wonder
at you no more.   290

FASHION

No? what wouldst thou say if a qualm of conscience should
spoil my design?

LORY

I would eat my words, and wonder more than ever.

FASHION

Why, faith, Lory, though I am a young rake-hell, and have
played many a roguish trick, this is so full-grown a cheat, I   295
find I must take pains to come up to't, I have scruples—

LORY

They are strong symptoms of death; if you find they increase, pray, sir, make your will.

FASHION

No, my conscience shan't starve me neither. But thus far
I will hearken to it, before I execute this project. I will try   300
my brother to the bottom, I'll speak to him with the temper
of a philosopher; my reasons (though they press him home)
shall yet be clothed with so much modesty, not one of all
the truths they urge shall be so naked to offend his sight. If
he has yet so much humanity about him as to assist me   305
(though with a moderate aid), I'll drop my project at his
feet, and show him I can do for him much more than what I
ask he'd do for me. This one conclusive trial of him I resolve
to make—

> Succeed or no, still victory's my lot;   310
> If I subdue his heart, 'tis well; if not,
> I shall subdue my conscience to my plot.

(Exeunt)

s.d. (*Exeunt*) Q1 follows this with 'The End of the First Act'.

Act II, Scene i
Enter LOVELESS *and* AMANDA

LOVELESS

How do you like these lodgings, my dear? For my part, I am
so well pleased with 'em, I shall hardly remove whilst we
stay in town, if you are satisfied.

AMANDA

I am satisfied with everything that pleases you; else I had
not come to town at all.   5

LOVELESS

Oh, a little of the noise and bustle of the world sweetens the
pleasures of retreat. We shall find the charms of our retirement doubled, when we return to it.

AMANDA

That pleasing prospect will be my chiefest entertainment,
whilst (much against my will) I am obliged to stand sur-   10
rounded with these empty pleasures, which 'tis so much the
fashion to be fond of.

LOVELESS

I own most of 'em are indeed but empty; nay, so empty, that
one would wonder by what magic power they act, when they
induce us to be vicious for their sakes. Yet some there are we   15
may speak kindlier of. There are delights (of which a private
life is destitute) which may divert an honest man, and be a
harmless entertainment to a virtuous woman. The conversation of the town is one; and truly (with some small allowances), the plays, I think, may be esteemed another.   20

AMANDA

The plays, I must confess, have some small charms; and
would have more, would they restrain that loose, obscene
encouragement to vice, which shocks, if not the virtue of
some woman, at least the modesty of all.

LOVELESS

But till that reformation can be made, I would not leave the   25
wholesome corn for some intruding tares that grow
amongst it. Doubtless the moral of a well-wrought scene is of
prevailing force. Last night there happened one that moved
me strangely.

AMANDA

Pray, what was that?   30

---

s.d. The scene is in Loveless's London lodgings.
  26 *corn . . . tares* The Scriptural paraphrase alerts us to hypocrisy.

LOVELESS
Why 'twas about—but 'tis not worth repeating.
AMANDA
Yes, pray let me know it.
LOVELESS
No; I think 'tis as well let alone.
AMANDA
Nay, now you make me have a mind to know.
LOVELESS
'Twas a foolish thing. You'd perhaps grow jealous should I   35
tell it you, though without cause, heaven knows.
AMANDA
I shall begin to think I have cause, if you persist in making
it a secret.
LOVELESS
I'll then convince you you have none, by making it no longer
so. Know then, I happened in the play to find 'my very   40
character, only with the addition of a relapse; which struck
me so, I put a sudden stop to a most harmless entertainment,
which till then diverted me between the acts. 'Twas to
admire the workmanship of nature, in the face of a young
lady that sat some distance from me, she was so exquisitely   45
handsome.
AMANDA
So exquisitely handsome?
LOVELESS
Why do you repeat my words, my dear?
AMANDA
Because you seemed to speak 'em with such pleasure, I
thought I might oblige you with their echo.   50
LOVELESS
Then you are alarmed, Amanda?
AMANDA
It is my duty to be so, when you are in danger.
LOVELESS
You are too quick in apprehending for me; all will be well
when you have heard me out. I do confess I gazed upon her;
nay, eagerly I gazed upon her.   55
AMANDA
Eagerly? that's with desire.
LOVELESS
No, I desired her not: I viewed her with a world of admira-
tion, but not one glance of love.

45 *sat* (CE) sate (Q1)

AMANDA

Take heed of trusting to such nice distinctions.

LOVELESS

I did take heed; for observing in the play that he who seemed   60
to represent me there was, by an accident like this, unwarily
surprised into a net, in which he lay a poor entangled slave,
and brought a train of mischiefs on his head, I snatched my
eyes away; they pleaded hard for leave to look again, but I
grew absolute, and they obeyed.   65

AMANDA

Were they the only things that were inquisitive? Had I been
in your place, my tongue, I fancy, had been curious, too;
I should have asked her name, and where she lived (yet still
without design). Who was she, pray?

LOVELESS

Indeed I cannot tell.   70

AMANDA

You will not tell.

LOVELESS

By all that's sacred then, I did not ask.

AMANDA

Nor do you know what company was with her?

LOVELESS

I do not.

AMANDA

Then I am calm again.   75

LOVELESS

Why were you disturbed?

AMANDA

Had I then no cause?

LOVELESS

None, certainly.

AMANDA

I thought I had.

LOVELESS

But you thought wrong, Amanda: for turn the case, and let   80
it be your story; should you come home, and tell me you
had seen a handsome man, should I grow jealous because
you had eyes?

AMANDA

But should I tell you he were exquisitely so; that I had
gazed on him with admiration; that I had looked with   85
eager eyes upon him; should you not think 'twere possible I
might go one step farther, and inquire his name?

LOVELESS

(*Aside*) She has reason on her side: I have talked too much;
but I must turn it off another way.

(*To* AMANDA) Will you then make no difference, Amanda,   90
between the language of our sex and yours? There is a
modesty restrains your tongues, which makes you speak by
halves when you commend; but roving flattery gives a loose
to ours, which makes us still speak double what we think.
You should not, therefore, in so strict a sense, take what I   95
said to her advantage.

AMANDA

Those flights of flattery, sir, are to our faces only: when
women once are out of hearing, you are as modest in our
commendations as we are. But I shan't put you to the trouble
of farther excuses; if you please this business shall rest here.   100
Only give me leave to wish, both for your peace and mine,
that you may never meet this miracle of beauty more.

LOVELESS

I am content.

Enter SERVANT

SERVANT

Madam, there's a young lady at the door in a chair, desires
to know whether your ladyship sees company. I think her   105
name is Berinthia.

AMANDA

O dear! 'tis a relation I have not seen these five years. Pray
her to walk in—(*Exit* SERVANT). (*To* LOVELESS) Here's
another beauty for you. She was young when I saw her last;
but I hear she's grown extremely handsome.   110

LOVELESS

Don't you be jealous now; for I shall gaze upon her, too.

Enter BERINTHIA

(*Aside*) Ha! By Heavens, the very woman!

BERINTHIA (*Saluting* AMANDA)

Dear Amanda, I did not expect to meet with you in town.

AMANDA

Sweet cousin, I'm overjoyed to see you. (*To* LOVELESS) Mr
Loveless, here's a relation and a friend of mine, I desire you'll   115
be better acquainted with.

LOVELESS (*Saluting* BERINTHIA)

If my wife never desires a harder thing, madam, her request
will be easily granted.

BERINTHIA (*To* AMANDA)

I think, madam, I ought to wish you joy.

AMANDA

Joy! Upon what?   120

BERINTHIA

Upon your marriage: you were a widow when I saw you last.

LOVELESS

You ought, rather, madam, to wish me joy upon that, since I am the only gainer.

BERINTHIA

If she has got so good a husband as the world reports, she has gained enough to expect the compliments of her friends   125 upon it.

LOVELESS

If the world is so favourable to me, to allow I deserve that title, I hope 'tis so just to my wife to own I derive it from her.

BERINTHIA

Sir, it is so just to you both, to own you are (and deserve to   130 be) the happiest pair that live in it.

LOVELESS

I'm afraid we shall lose that character, madam, whenever you happen to change your condition.

Enter SERVANT

SERVANT

Sir, my Lord Foppington presents his humble service to you, and desires to know how you do. He but just now heard   135 you were in town. He's at the next door; and if it be not inconvenient, he'll come and wait upon you.

LOVELESS

Lord Foppington!—I know him not.

BERINTHIA

Not his dignity, perhaps, but you do his person. 'Tis Sir Novelty; he has bought a barony, in order to marry a great   140 fortune. His patent has not been passed eight-and-forty hours, and he has already sent how-do-ye's to all the town, to make 'em acquainted with his title.

LOVELESS

Give my service to his lordship, and let him know I am proud of the honour he intends me. (*Exit* [SERVANT]) Sure this   145

121 *a widow when I saw you last* Cf. *Love's Last Shift,* I. iii, '*Enter* Hillaria, Narcissa, *and* Amanda, *in mourning*'.
127 *If the* (CE) I the (Q1)

addition of quality must have so improved his coxcomb, he
can't but be very good company for a quarter of an hour.

AMANDA

Now it moves my pity more than my mirth, to see a man
whom nature has made no fool, be so very industrious to
pass for an ass.   150

LOVELESS

No, there you are wrong, Amanda; you should never bestow
your pity upon those who take pains for your contempt.
Pity those whom nature abuses, but never those who abuse
nature.

BERINTHIA

Besides, the town would be robbed of one of its chief   155
diversions if it should become a crime to laugh at a fool.

AMANDA

I could never yet perceive the town inclined to part with any
of its diversions, for the sake of their being crimes; but I
have seen it very fond of some I think had little else to
recommend 'em.   160

BERINTHIA

I doubt, Amanda, you are grown its enemy, you speak with
so much warmth against it.

AMANDA

I must confess I am not much its friend.

BERINTHIA

Then give me leave to make you mine, but not engaging in
its quarrel.   165

AMANDA

You have many stronger claims than that, Berinthia, whenever you think fit to plead your title.

LOVELESS

You have done well to engage a second, my dear; for here
comes one will be apt to call you to an account for your
country principles.   170

Enter LORD FOPPINGTON

LORD FOPPINGTON (*To* LOVELESS)

Sir, I am your most humble servant.

LOVELESS

I wish you joy, my lord.

LORD FOPPINGTON

O Lard, sir—Madam, your ladyship's welcome to tawn.

AMANDA

I wish your lordship joy.

3 * *

LORD FOPPINGTON

O Heavens, madam—   175

LOVELESS

My lord, this young lady is a relation of my wife's.

LORD FOPPINGTON (*Saluting* BERINTHIA)

The beautifullest race of people upon earth, rat me! Dear
Loveless, I'm overjoyed to see you have braught your family
to tawn again; I am, stap my vitals!—(*Aside*) Far I design
to lie with your wife.—(*To* AMANDA) Far Gad's sake,   180
madam, haw has your ladyship been able to subsist thus
long, under the fatigue of a country life?

AMANDA

My life has been very far from that, my lord; it has been
a very quiet one.

LORD FOPPINGTON

Why, that's the fatigue I speak of, madam. For 'tis im-   185
possible to be quiet, without thinking: now thinking is to
me the greatest fatigue in the world.

AMANDA

Does not your lordship love reading then?

LORD FOPPINGTON

Oh, passionately, madam.—But I never think of what I
read.   190

BERINTHIA

Why, how can your lordship read without thinking?

LORD FOPPINGTON

O Lard!—can your ladyship pray without devotion, madam?

AMANDA

Well, I must own I think books the best entertainment in the
world.

LORD FOPPINGTON

I am so very much of your ladyship's mind, madam, that I   195
have a private gallery (where I walk sometimes) is furnished
with nothing but books and looking-glasses. Madam, I have
gilded 'em, and ranged 'em so prettily, before Gad, it is the
most entertaining thing in the world to walk and look upon
'em.   200

AMANDA

Nay, I love a neat library, too; but 'tis, I think, the inside
of the book should recommend it most to us.

LORD FOPPINGTON

That, I must confess, I am nat altogether so fand of. Far to

177 s.d. BERINTHIA ed. her (Q1)

mind the inside of a book, is to entertain one's self with the
forced product of another man's brain. Naw I think a man of   205
quality and breeding may be much better diverted with the
natural sprauts of his own. But to say the truth, madam, let
a man love reading never so well, when once he comes to
know this tawn, he finds so many better ways of passing
the four-and-twenty hours, that 'twere ten thousand pities   210
he should consume his time in that. Far example, madam,
my life; my life, madam, is a perpetual stream of pleasure,
that glides through such a variety of entertainments, I believe
the wisest of our ancestors never had the least conception of
any of 'em.   215

I rise, madam, about ten a-clock. I don't rise sooner,
because 'tis the worst thing in the world for the complexion;
nat that I pretend to be a beau; but a man must endeavour
to look wholesome, lest he make so nauseous a figure in the
side-bax, the ladies should be compelled to turn their eyes   220
upon the play. So at ten a-clack, I say, I rise. Naw, if I find
'tis a good day, I resalve to take a turn in the Park, and see
the fine women; so huddle on my clothes, and get dressed by
one. If it be nasty weather, I take a turn in the chocolate-
hause: where, as you walk, madam, you have the prettiest   225
prospect in the world; you have looking-glasses all round
you.—But I'm afraid I tire the company.

BERINTHIA
Not at all. Pray go on.

LORD FOPPINGTON
Why then, ladies, from thence I go to dinner at Lacket's,
where you are so nicely and delicately served, that, stap my   230
vitals, they shall compose you a dish no bigger than a saucer,
shall come to fifty shillings. Between eating my dinner (and
washing my mauth, ladies) I spend my time, till I go to the
play; where, till nine a-clack, I entertain myself with looking
upon the company, and usually dispose of one hour more   235
in leading 'em aut. So there's twelve of the four-and-
twenty pretty well over. The other twelve, madam, are
disposed of in two articles: in the first four I toast myself
drunk, and in t'other eight I sleep myself sober again. Thus,
ladies, you see my life is an eternal raund O of delights.   240

216, 226 *clock, round* Possibly the compositor could not keep up with
    the consistency of the alteration of 'o' to 'a' in Foppington's
    speech; but in Q1 these probable actor's 'a's are printed as 'o's.
233–4 *go to the play* The play usually commenced before six in that
    period.   240 *raund O of delights* i.e. round circle

LOVELESS

'Tis a heavenly one indeed.

AMANDA

But I thought, my lord, you beaux spent a great deal of your time in intrigues: you have given us no account of them yet.

LORD FOPPINGTON (*Aside*)

Soh, she would inquire into my amours—That's jealousy— She begins to be in love with me—(*To* AMANDA) Why, 245 madam—as to time for my intrigues, I usually make detachments of it from my other pleasures, according to the exigency. Far your ladyship may please to take notice, that those who intrigue with women of quality, have rarely occasion far above half an hour at a time: people of that 250 rank being under those decorums, they can seldom give you a langer view than will just serve to shoot 'em flying. So that the course of my other pleasures is not very much interrupted by my amours.

LOVELESS

But your lordship is now become a pillar of the state; you 255 must attend the weighty affairs of the nation.

LORD FOPPINGTON

Sir,—as to weighty affairs, I leave them to weighty heads. I never intend mine shall be a burden to my body.

LOVELESS

Oh, but you'll find the House will expect your attendance.

LORD FOPPINGTON

Sir, you'll find the House will compound for my appearance. 260

LOVELESS

But your friends will take it ill if you don't attend their particular causes.

LORD FOPPINGTON

Not, sir, if I come time enough to give 'em my particular vote.

BERINTHIA

But pray, my lord, how do you dispose of yourself on 265 Sundays? For that, methinks, is a day should hang wretchedly upon your hands.

LORD FOPPINGTON

Why, faith, madam—Sunday—is a vile day, I must confess. I intend to move for leave to bring in a bill, that the players may work upon it, as well as the hackney coaches. Though 270 this I must say for the government, it leaves us the churches

260 *compound* mutually agree about

to entertain us.—But then again, they begin so abominable
early, a man must rise by candle-light to get dressed by the
psalm.

BERINTHIA

Pray which church does your lordship most oblige with   275
your presence?

LORD FOPPINGTON

Oh, St James's madam;—there's much the best company.

AMANDA

Is there good preaching, too?

LORD FOPPINGTON

Why, faith, madam—I can't tell. A man must have very
little to do there that can give an account of the sermon.   280

BERINTHIA

You can give us an account of the ladies at least?

LORD FOPPINGTON

Or I deserve to be excommunicated.—There is my Lady
Tattle, my Lady Prate, my Lady Titter, my Lady Leer, my
Lady Giggle, and my Lady Grin. These sit in the front of
the boxes, and all church-time are the prettiest company in   285
the world, stap my vitals.—(*To* AMANDA) Mayn't we hope for
the honour to see your ladyship added to our society,
madam?

AMANDA

Alas, my lord, I am the worst company in the world at
church: I'm apt to mind the prayers, or the sermon, or—   290

LORD FOPPINGTON

One is indeed strangely apt at church to mind what one
should not do. But I hope, madam, at one time or other, I
shall have the honour to lead your ladyship to your coach
there.—(*Aside*) Methinks she seems strangely pleased with
everything I say to her. 'Tis a vast pleasure to receive   295
encouragement from a woman before her husband's face.
—I have a good mind to pursue my conquest, and speak the
thing plainly to her at once. Egad, I'll do't, and that in so
cavalier a manner, she shall be surprised at it. [*Aloud*]
Ladies, I'll take my leave; I'm afraid I begin to grow   300
troublesome with the length of my visit.

AMANDA

Your lordship's too entertaining to grow troublesome anywhere.

277 *St James's* St James, Piccadilly

LORD FOPPINGTON (*Aside*)

    That now was as much as if she had said—pray lie with me.
    I'll let her see I'm quick of apprehension.—(*To* AMANDA)   305
    O Lard, madam, I had like to have forgot a secret, I must
    needs tell your ladyship.—(*To* LOVELESS) Ned, you must
    not be so jealous now as to listen.

LOVELESS

    Not I, my lord, I am too fashionable a husband to pry into
    the secrets of my wife.   310

LORD FOPPINGTON (*To* AMANDA, *squeezing her hand*)

    I am in love with you to desperation, strike me speechless!

AMANDA (*Giving him a box o'the ear*)

    Then thus I return your passion.—An impudent fool!

LORD FOPPINGTON

    Gad's curse, madam, I'm a peer of the realm!

LOVELESS

    Hey, what the devil, do you affront my wife, sir? Nay then—
    (*They draw and fight. The women run shrieking for help*)

AMANDA

    Ah! What has my folly done? Help! Murder! Help! part 'em,   315
    for heaven's sake!

LORD FOPPINGTON (*Falling back and leaning upon his sword*)

    Ah—quite through the body!—stap my vitals!

Enter SERVANTS

LOVELESS (*Running to him*)

    I hope I han't killed the fool however.—Bear him up!—
    Where's your wound?

LORD FOPPINGTON

    Just through the guts.   320

LOVELESS

    Call a surgeon there.—Unbutton him quickly.

LORD FOPPINGTON

    Ay, pray make haste.

                                   [*Exit* SERVANT]

LOVELESS

    This mischief you may thank yourself for.

LORD FOPPINGTON

    I may so—love's the devil indeed, Ned.

Enter SYRINGE *and* SERVANT

SERVANT

    Here's Mr Syringe, sir, was just going by the door.   325

325 *Syringe* ed. and s.d. (Seringe (Q1))

LORD FOPPINGTON

He's the welcomest man alive.

SYRINGE

Stand by, stand by, stand by! Pray, gentlemen, stand by.
Lord have mercy upon us! did you never see a man run
through the body before? Pray, stand by!

LORD FOPPINGTON

Ah, Mr Syringe—I'm a dead man! 330

SYRINGE

A dead man and I by! I should laugh to see that, egad!

LOVELESS

Prithee don't stand prating, but look upon his wound.

SYRINGE

Why, what if I won't look upon his wound this hour, sir?

LOVELESS

Why, then he'll bleed to death, sir.

SYRINGE

Why, then I'll fetch him to life again, sir. 335

LOVELESS

'Slife, he's run through the guts, I tell thee.

SYRINGE

Would he were run through the heart, I should get the
more credit by his cure. Now I hope you're satisfied? Come,
now, let me come at him; now let me come at him. (*Viewing
his wound*) Oons, what a gash is here!—Why, sir, a man may 340
drive a coach and six horses into your body.

LORD FOPPINGTON

Ho!

SYRINGE

Why, what the devil, have you run the gentleman through
with a scythe?—(*Aside*) A little prick between the skin and
the ribs, that's all. 345

LOVELESS

Let me see his wound.

SYRINGE

Then you shall dress it, sir; for if anybody looks upon it,
I won't.

LOVELESS

Why, thou art the veriest coxcomb I ever saw.

SYRINGE

Sir, I am not master of my trade for nothing. 350

LORD FOPPINGTON

Surgeon!

SYRINGE

Well, sir.

LORD FOPPINGTON

Is there any hopes?

SYRINGE

Hopes? I can't tell. What are you willing to give for your
cure?   355

LORD FOPPINGTON

Five hundred paunds, with pleasure.

SYRINGE

Why, then perhaps there may be hopes. But we must avoid
farther delay.—Here; help the gentleman into a chair, and
carry him to my house presently, that's the properest place
—(*Aside*) to bubble him out of his money.—[*Aloud*] Come,   360
a chair, a chair quickly—there, in with him.

> (*They put him into a chair*)

LORD FOPPINGTON

Dear Loveless—adieu! If I die—I forgive thee; and if I
live—I hope thou'lt do as much by me. I'm very sorry you
and I should quarrel; but I hope here's an end on't, for if
you are satisfied—I am.   365

LOVELESS

I shall hardly think it worth my prosecuting any farther, so
you may be at rest, sir.

LORD FOPPINGTON

Thou art a generous fellow, strike me dumb.—(*Aside*) But
thou hast an impertinent wife, stap my vitals.

SYRINGE

So, carry him off, carry him off, we shall have him prate   370
himself into a fever by and by; carry him off!

> (*Exit* SYRINGE *with* LORD FOPPINGTON)

AMANDA

Now on my knees, my dear, let me ask your pardon for my
indiscretion, my own I never shall obtain.

LOVELESS

Oh, there's no harm done: you served him well.

AMANDA

He did indeed deserve it. But I tremble to think how dear   375
my indiscreet resentment might have cost you.

LOVELESS

Oh, no matter, never trouble yourself about that.

360 *bubble* cheat

BERINTHIA

For heaven's sake, what was't he did to you?

AMANDA

Oh, nothing; he only squeezed me kindly by the hand, and
frankly offered me a coxcomb's heart. I know I was to blame   380
to resent it as I did, since nothing but a quarrel could
ensue. But the fool so surprised me with his insolence, I
was not mistress of my fingers.

BERINTHIA

Now, I dare swear, he thinks you had 'em at great command, they obeyed you so readily.   385

Enter WORTHY

WORTHY

Save you, save you, good people: I'm glad to find you all
alive; I met a wounded peer carrying off. For heaven's sake,
what was the matter?

LOVELESS

Oh, a trifle! He would have lain with my wife before my
face, so she obliged him with a box o' th'ear, and I run him   390
through the body: that was all.

WORTHY

Bagatelle on all sides. But, pray, madam, how long has this
noble lord been an humble servant of yours?

AMANDA

This is the first I have heard on't. So I suppose 'tis his
quality more than his love has brought him into this   395
adventure. He thinks his title an authentic passport to every
woman's heart below the degree of a peeress.

WORTHY

He's coxcomb enough to think anything. But I would not
have you brought into trouble for him. I hope there's no
danger of his life?   400

LOVELESS

None at all. He's fallen into the hands of a roguish surgeon,
[who] I perceive designs to frighten a little money out of
him. But I saw his wound, 'tis nothing; he may go to the
play tonight, if he pleases.

WORTHY

I am glad you have corrected him without farther mischief.   405
And now, sir, if these ladies have no farther service for you,
you'll oblige me if you can go to the place I spoke to you of
t'other day.

LOVELESS

With all my heart.—(*Aside*) Though I could wish, methinks, to stay and gaze a little longer on that creature. Good gods, how beautiful she is!—But what have I to do with beauty? I have already had my portion, and must not covet more. (*To* WORTHY) Come, sir, when you please.

WORTHY

Ladies, your servant.

AMANDA

Mr Loveless, pray one word with you before you go.   415

LOVELESS (*To* WORTHY)

I'll overtake you, sir.   (*Exit* WORTHY)
What would my dear?

AMANDA

Only a woman's foolish question—how do you like my cousin here?

LOVELESS

Jealous already, Amanda?   420

AMANDA

Not at all, I ask you for another reason.

LOVELESS (*Aside*)

Whate'er her reason be, I must not tell her true.
—(*To* AMANDA) Why, I confess she's handsome. But you must not think I slight your kinswoman, if I own to you, of all the women who may claim that character, she is the   425
last would triumph in my heart.

AMANDA

I'm satisfied.

LOVELESS

Now tell me why you asked?

AMANDA

At night I will. Adieu.

LOVELESS (*Kissing her*)

I'm yours.   (*Exit* LOVELESS)   430

AMANDA (*Aside*)

I'm glad to find he does not like her, for I have a great mind to persuade her to come and live with me.—(*To* BERINTHIA) Now, dear Berinthia, let me inquire a little into your affairs: for I do assure you, I am enough your friend to interest myself in everything that concerns you.   435

BERINTHIA

You formerly have given me such proofs on't, I should be very much to blame to doubt it. I am sorry I have no secrets

to trust you with, that I might convince you how entire a
confidence I durst repose in you.

AMANDA

Why, is it possible that one so young and beautiful as you   440
should live and have no secrets?

BERINTHIA

What secrets do you mean?

AMANDA

Lovers.

BERINTHIA

Oh, twenty! but not one secret amongst 'em. Lovers in this
age have too much honour to do anything underhand; they   445
do all above board.

AMANDA

That now, methinks, would make me hate a man.

BERINTHIA

But the women of the town are of another mind: for by this
means a lady may (with the expense of a few coquette
glances) lead twenty fools about in a string for two or three   450
years together. Whereas if she should allow 'em greater
favours, and oblige 'em to secrecy, she would not keep one
of 'em a fortnight.

AMANDA

There's something indeed in that to satisfy the vanity of a
woman, but I can't comprehend how the men find their   455
account in it.

BERINTHIA

Their entertainment, I must confess, is a riddle to me. For
there's very few of 'em ever get farther than a bow and an
ogle. I have half a score for my share, who follow me all
over the town; and at the play, the park, and the church,   460
do (with their eyes) say the violentest things to me.—But I
never hear any more of 'em.

AMANDA

What can be the reason of that?

BERINTHIA

One reason is, they don't know how to go farther. They have
had so little practice, they don't understand the trade. But,   465
besides their ignorance, you must know there is not one of
my half score lovers but what follows half a score mistresses.
Now, their affections being divided amongst so many, are not
strong enough for any one to make 'em pursue her to the
purpose. Like a young puppy in a warren, they have a flirt   470
at all and catch none.

AMANDA

Yet they seem to have a torrent of love to dispose of.

BERINTHIA

They have so. But 'tis like the rivers of a modern philosopher,
(whose works, though a woman, I have read), it sets out
with a violent stream, splits in a thousand branches, and is   475
all lost in the sands.

AMANDA

But do you think this river of love runs all its course without doing any mischief? Do you think it overflows nothing?

BERINTHIA

Oh yes; 'tis true it never breaks into anybody's ground that
has the least fence about it; but it overflows all the commons   480
that lie in its way. And this is the utmost achievement of
those dreadful champions in the field of love—the beaux.

AMANDA

But prithee, Berinthia, instruct me a little farther, for I'm
so great a novice I am almost ashamed on't. My husband's
leaving me whilst I was young and fond threw me into that   485
depth of discontent, that ever since I have led so private and
recluse a life, my ignorance is scarce conceivable. I therefore
fain would be instructed. Not (Heaven knows) that what
you call intrigues have any charms for me; my love and
principles are too well fixed. The practic part of all unlawful   490
love is—

BERINTHIA

Oh, 'tis abominable! But for the speculative, that we must
all confess is entertaining. The conversation of all the
virtuous women in the town turns upon that and new
clothes.   495

AMANDA

Pray be so just then to me, to believe, 'tis with a world of
innocency I would inquire, whether you think those women
we call women of reputation, do really 'scape all other men,
as they do those shadows of 'em, the beaux.

BERINTHIA

Oh no, Amanda; there are a sort of men make dreadful work   500
amongst 'em, men that may be called the beaux' antipathy,

473 *philosopher* Zimansky notes that Berinthia refers to Thomas
   Burnet's *The Sacred Theory of the Earth* (1684), Bk. II Ch. V., a
   translation of the first two books of Burnet's *Telluris Theoria
   Sacra* (1681).
499 *shadows* a neat use of the old commonplace that women are but
   men's shadows

for they agree in nothing but walking upon two legs.—These
have brains; the beau has none. These are in love with their
mistress; the beau with himself. They take care of her
reputation; he's industrious to destroy it. They are decent;   505
he's a fop. They are sound; he's rotten. They are men;
he's an ass.

AMANDA

If this be their character, I fancy we had here e'en now a
pattern of 'em both.

BERINTHIA

His lordship and Mr Worthy?   510

AMANDA

The same.

BERINTHIA

As for the lord, he's eminently so; and for the other, I can
assure you, there's not a man in town who has a better
interest with the women, that are worth having an interest
with. But 'tis all private: he's like a back-stair minister at   515
court, who, whilst the reputed favourites are sauntering in
the bed-chamber, is ruling the roost in the closet.

AMANDA

He answers then the opinion I had ever of him. Heavens,
what a difference there is between a man like him, and that
vain nauseous fop, Sir Novelty—(*Taking her hand*) I must   520
acquaint you with a secret, cousin. 'Tis not that fool alone has
talked to me of love. Worthy has been tampering too. 'Tis
true, he has done't in vain: not all his charms or art have
power to shake me. My love, my duty, and my virtue, are
such faithful guards, I need not fear my heart should e'er   525
betray me. But what I wonder at is this: I find I did not start
at this proposal, as when it came from one whom I con-
temned. I therefore mention this attempt, that I may learn
from you whence it proceeds; that vice (which cannot change
its nature) should so far change at least its shape, as that the   530
self-same crime proposed from one shall seem a monster
gaping at your ruin; when from another it shall look so kind,
as though it were your friend, and never meant to harm
you. Whence, think you, can this difference proceed? For
'tis not love, heaven knows.   535

517 *bed-chamber . . . closet* The distinction depends upon our remem-
    bering that a monarch's bed-chamber was in public use for levees,
    whereas his closet was a place of personal privacy.
528 *this* his (Q1 copy-text, CE and 1735) but Zimansky notes a
    dropped t in some copies of Q1 and the reading is preferable

BERINTHIA

Oh no, I would not for the world ·believe it were. But
possibly, should there a dreadful sentence pass upon you, to
undergo the rage of both their passions, the pain you'd
apprehend from one might seem so trivial to the other, the
danger would not quite so much alarm you.   540

AMANDA

Fie, fie, Berinthia! you would indeed alarm me, could you
incline me to a thought that all the merit of mankind com-
bined could shake that tender love I bear my husband. No!
he sits triumphant in my heart, and nothing can dethrone
him.   545

BERINTHIA

But should he abdicate again, do you think you should
preserve the vacant throne ten tedious winters more in
hopes of his return?

AMANDA

Indeed, I think I should. Though I confess, after those
obligations he has to me, should he abandon me once more,   550
my heart would grow extremely urgent with me to root him
thence, and cast him out forever.

BERINTHIA

Were I that thing they call a slighted wife, somebody should
run the risk of being that thing they call—a husband.

AMANDA

O fie, Berinthia! no revenge should ever be taken against a   555
husband. But to wrong his bed is a vengeance, which of all
vengeance—

BERINTHIA

Is the sweetest. Ha! ha! ha! Don't I talk madly?

AMANDA

Madly, indeed.

BERINTHIA

Yet I'm very innocent.   560

AMANDA

That I dare swear you are. I know how to make allowances
for your humour. You were always very entertaining company; but I find since marriage and widowhood have shown
you the world a little, you are very much improved.

BERINTHIA (*Aside*)

Alack a-day, there has gone more than that to improve me, if   565
she knew all!

554 *husband* Amanda is quick to recognise that Berinthia means a
    cuckold.

AMANDA

For heaven's sake, Berinthia, tell me what way I shall take to
persuade you to come and live with me?

BERINTHIA

Why, one way in the world there is—and but one.

AMANDA

Pray which is that?   570

BERINTHIA

It is, to assure me—I shall be very welcome.

AMANDA

If that be all, you shall e'en lie here tonight.

BERINTHIA

Tonight?

AMANDA

Yes, tonight.

BERINTHIA

Why, the people where I lodge will think me mad.   575

AMANDA

Let 'em think what they please.

BERINTHIA

Say you so, Amanda? Why, then they shall think what they
please: for I'm a young widow, and I care not what anybody thinks. Ah, Amanda, it's a delicious thing to be a
young widow!   580

AMANDA

You'll hardly make me think so.

BERINTHIA

Puh! because you are in love with your husband: but that is
not every woman's case.

AMANDA

I hope 'twas yours, at least.

BERINTHIA

Mine, say ye? Now have I a great mind to tell you a lie, but I 585
should do it so awkwardly you'd find me out.

AMANDA

Then e'en speak the truth.

BERINTHIA

Shall I?—Then after all I did love him, Amanda—as a nun
does penance.

AMANDA

Why did not you refuse to marry him, then?   590

BERINTHIA

Because my mother would have whipped me.

AMANDA

How did you live together?

BERINTHIA

Like man and wife, asunder. He loved the country, I the
town. He hawks and hounds, I coaches and equipage. He
eating and drinking, I carding and playing. He the sound of 595
a horn, I the squeak of a fiddle. We were dull company at
table, worse a-bed. Whenever we met, we gave one another
the spleen; and never agreed but once, which was about
lying alone.

AMANDA

But tell me one thing, truly and sincerely.   600

BERINTHIA

What's that?

AMANDA

Notwithstanding all these jars, did not his death at last
extremely trouble you?

BERINTHIA

Oh yes. Not that my present pangs were so very violent,
but the after-pains were intolerable. I was forced to wear   605
a beastly widow's band a twelvemonth for't.

AMANDA

Women, I find, have different inclinations.

BERINTHIA

Women, I find, keep different company. When your husband
ran away from you, if you had fallen into some of my
acquaintance, 'twould have saved you many a tear. But you   610
go and live with a grandmother, a bishop, and an old nurse;
which was enough to make any woman break her heart for
her husband. Pray, Amanda, if ever you are a widow again,
keep yourself so, as I do.

AMANDA

Why, do you then resolve you'll never marry?   615

BERINTHIA

Oh no, I resolve I will.

AMANDA

How so?

BERINTHIA

That I never may.

AMANDA

You banter me.

BERINTHIA

Indeed I don't. But I consider I'm a woman, and form my   620
resolutions accordingly.

AMANDA
  Well, my opinion is, form what resolution you will,
  matrimony will be the end on't.
BERINTHIA
  Faith it won't.
AMANDA
  How do you know?   625
BERINTHIA
  I'm sure on't.
AMANDA
  Why, do you think 'tis impossible for you to fall in love?
BERINTHIA
  No.
AMANDA
  Nay, but to grow so passionately fond, that nothing but the
  man you love can give you rest.   630
BERINTHIA
  Well, what then?
AMANDA
  Why, then you'll marry him.
BERINTHIA
  How do you know that?
AMANDA
  Why, what can you do else?
BERINTHIA
  Nothing—but sit and cry.   635
AMANDA
  Psha!
BERINTHIA
  Ah, poor Amanda! you have led a country life: but if you'll
  consult the widows of this town, they'll tell you you should
  never take a lease of a house you can hire for a quarter's
  warning.   640

                                                      (*Exeunt*)

Act III, Scene i

Enter LORD FOPPINGTON *and* SERVANT

LORD FOPPINGTON
  Hey, fellow, let the coach come to the door.

640 *warning* note of tenancy
s.d. (*Exeunt*) Q1 follows this with 'The End of the Second act'.
  1 *door* The location is obviously Lord Foppington's house.

SERVANT

Will your lordship venture so soon to expose yourself to the weather?

LORD FOPPINGTON

Sir, I will venture as soon as I can, to expose myself to the ladies; though give me my cloak, however; for in that side-box, what between the air that comes in at the door on one side, and the intolerable warmth of the masks on t'other, a man gets so many heats and colds, 'twould destroy the canstitution of a harse. 5

SERVANT (*Putting on his cloak*)

I wish your lordship would please to keep house a little longer; I'm afraid your honour does not well consider your wound. 10

LORD FOPPINGTON

My wound!—I would not be in eclipse another day, though I had as many wounds in my guts as I have had in my heart.

[*Exit* SERVANT]

Enter YOUNG FASHION

FASHION

Brother, your servant. How do you find yourself today? 15

LORD FOPPINGTON

So well, that I have ardered my coach to the door: so there's no great danger of death this baut, Tam.

FASHION

I'm very glad of it.

LORD FOPPINGTON (*Aside*)

That I believe's a lie.—[*Aloud*] Prithee, Tam, tell me one thing: did nat your heart cut a caper up to your mauth, when you heard I was run through the bady? 20

FASHION

Why do you think it should?

LORD FOPPINGTON

Because I remember mine did so, when I heard my father was shat through the head.

FASHION

It then did very ill. 25

LORD FOPPINGTON

Prithee, why so?

FASHION

Because he used you very well.

---

7 *masks* Dobrée notes that masks were not worn by respectable women in this period.

LORD FOPPINGTON

Well?—Naw strike me dumb! he starved me. He has let me
want a thausand women for want of a thausand paund.

FASHION

Then he hindered you from making a great many ill bargains,   30
for I think no woman is worth money that will take money.

LORD FOPPINGTON

If I were a younger brother, I should think so too.

FASHION

Why, is it possible you can value a woman that's to be
bought?

LORD FOPPINGTON

Prithee, why not as well as a padnag?   35

FASHION

Because a woman has a heart to dispose of; a horse has
none.

LORD FOPPINGTON

Look you, Tam, of all things that belang to a woman, I have
an aversion to her heart. Far when once a woman has given
you her heart, you can never get rid of the rest of her body.   40

FASHION

This is strange doctrine. But pray in your amours how is it
with your own heart?

LORD FOPPINGTON

Why, my heart in my amours—is like—my heart aut of my
amours; à la glace. My bady, Tam, is a watch; and my
heart is the pendulum to it; whilst the finger runs raund to   45
every hour in the circle, that still beats the same time.

FASHION

Then you are seldom much in love?

LORD FOPPINGTON

Never, stap my vitals.

FASHION

Why then did you make all this bustle about Amanda?

LORD FOPPINGTON

Because she was a woman of an insolent virtue, and I   50
thought myself piqued in honour to debauch her.

FASHION

Very well.—(Aside) Here's a rare fellow for you, to have the

35 padnag easy-going, rather than high-spirited, animal; cf.
   O.E.D.'s example from Macaulay, History of England, vii, II, 172,
   'To procure an easy padnag for his wife'. Foppington possibly puns
   on 'baggage' and 'hire' since he is talking about whores.
51 piqued (1735) pickt (Q1)

spending of five thousand pounds a year! But now for my
business with him.—(*To* LORD FOPPINGTON) Brother,
though I know to talk to you of business (especially of   55
money) is a theme not quite so entertaining to you as that
of the ladies, my necessities are such, I hope you'll have
patience to hear me.

LORD FOPPINGTON

The greatness of your necessities, Tam, is the worst argument in the world for your being patiently heard. I do   60
believe you are going to make me a very good speech, but,
strike me dumb! it has the worst beginning of any speech I
have heard this twelvemonth.

FASHION

I'm very sorry you think so.

LORD FOPPINGTON

I do believe thau art. But come, let's know thy affair quickly;   65
far 'tis a new play, and I shall be so rumpled and squeezed
with pressing through the crawd, to get to my servant, the
women will think I have lain all night in my clothes.

FASHION

Why, then (that I may not be the author of so great a misfortune) my case in a word is this. The necessary expenses   70
of my travels have so much exceeded the wretched income
of my annuity, that I have been forced to mortgage it for
five hundred pounds, which is spent; so that unless you are
so kind to assist me in redeeming it, I know no remedy but
to go take a purse.   75

LORD FOPPINGTON

Why, faith, Tam—to give you my sense of the thing, I do
think taking a purse the best remedy in the world: for if
you succeed, you are relieved that way; if you are taken—you
are relieved t'other.

FASHION

I'm glad to see you are in so pleasant a humour. I hope I   80
shall find the effects on't.

LORD FOPPINGTON

Why, do you then really think it a reasonable thing I should
give you five hundred paunds?

FASHION

I do not ask it as a due, brother, I am willing to receive it
as a favour.   85

LORD FOPPINGTON

Thau art willing to receive it anyhaw, strike me speechless!
But these are damned times to give money in, taxes are so

great, repairs so exorbitant, tenants such rogues, and
periwigs so dear, that the devil take me, I am reduced to that
extremity in my cash, I have been forced to retrench in that   90
one article of sweet pawder, till I have braught it dawn to
five guineas a manth. Naw judge, Tam, whether I can spare
you five hundred paunds.

FASHION

If you can't, I must starve, that's all.—(*Aside*) Damn him!

LORD FOPPINGTON

All I can say is, you should have been a better husband.   95

FASHION

Oons, if you can't live upon five thousand a year, how do you
think I should do't upon two hundred?

LORD FOPPINGTON

Don't be in a passion, Tam; far passion is the most un-
becoming thing in the world—to the face. Look you, I don't
love to say anything to you to make you melancholy; but   100
upon this occasion I must take leave to put you in mind that
a running horse does require more attendance than a coach-
horse. Nature has made some difference 'twixt you and I.

FASHION

Yes, she has made you older—(*Aside*) Pox take her!

LORD FOPPINGTON

That is nat all, Tam.   105

FASHION

Why, what is there else?

LORD FOPPINGTON (*Looking first upon himself, then upon his
brother*)

Ask the ladies.

FASHION

Why, thou essence bottle! thou musk cat! dost thou then
think thou hast any advantage over me but what Fortune
has given thee?   110

LORD FOPPINGTON

I do—stap my vitals!

FASHION

Now, by all that's great and powerful, thou art the prince
of coxcombs!

---

95 *husband* husbander of your resources
102 *running horse* racehorse
108 *essence* scent *musk* a main source of perfume

LORD FOPPINGTON

Sir—I am praud of being at the head of so prevailing a party.

FASHION

Will nothing then provoke thee? Draw, coward!   115

LORD FOPPINGTON

Look you, Tam, you know I have always taken you for a
mighty dull fellow, and here is one of the foolishest plats
broke out that I have seen a long time. Your paverty makes
your life so burdensome to you, you would provoke me to a
quarrel, in hopes either to slip through my lungs into my   120
estate, or to get yourself run through the guts, to put an
end to your pain. But I will disappoint you in both your
designs; far, with the temper of a philasapher, and the dis-
cretion of a statesman—I will go to the play with my sword
in my scabbard.   (*Exit*) 125

FASHION

Soh! Farewell, snuff-box! And now, conscience, I defy thee.
—Lory!

Enter LORY

LORY

Sir.

FASHION

Here's rare news, Lory; his lordship has given me a pill
has purged off all my scruples.   130

LORY

Then my heart's at ease again. For I have been in a lament-
able fright, sir, ever since your conscience had the impudence
to intrude into your company.

FASHION

Be at peace, it will come there no more: my brother has given
it a wring by the nose, and I have kicked it down stairs. So   135
run away to the inn; get the horses ready quickly, and bring
'em to old Coupler's, without a moment's delay.

LORY

Then sir, you are going straight about the fortune?

FASHION

I am. Away! fly, Lory!

LORY

The happiest day I ever saw. I'm upon the wing already.   140

(*Exeunt several ways*)

114 *Sir . . . party* One of Foppington's finest lines, drawn from the
     dangerously witty truth of the beaux as a third force in party
     politics.

Act III, Scene ii

A Garden
Enter LOVELESS *and* SERVANT

LOVELESS
  Is my wife within?
SERVANT
  No, sir, she has been gone out this half hour.
LOVELESS
  'Tis well, leave me.   [*Exit* SERVANT]
                    Solus
  Sure Fate has yet some business to be done,
  Before Amanda's heart and mine must rest;   5
  Else, why amongst those legions of her sex,
  Which throng the world,
  Should she pick out for her companion
  The only one on earth
  Whom nature has endow'd for her undoing?   10
  Undoing, was't I said—who shall undo her?
  Is not her empire fix'd? am I not hers?
  Did she not rescue me, a grovelling slave,
  When chained and bound by that black tyrant vice,
  I laboured in his vilest drudgery?   15
  Did she not ransom me, and set me free?
  Nay, more: when by my follies sunk
  To a poor, tattered, despicable beggar,
  Did she not lift me up to envied fortune?
  Give me herself, and all that she possessed,   20
  Without a thought of more return,
  Than what a poor repenting heart might make her?
  Han't she done this? And if she has,
  Am I not strongly bound to love her for it?
  To love her!—Why, do I not love her then?   25
  By Earth and Heaven I do!
  Nay, I have demonstration that I do:
  For I would sacrifice my life to serve her.
  Yet hold—if laying down my life
  Be demonstration of my love,   30
  What is't I feel in favour of Berinthia?
  For should she be in danger, methinks I could incline to risk
  it for her service too; and yet I do not love her. How then
  subsists my proof?—Oh, I have found it out! What I would
  do for one, is demonstration of my love; and if I'd do as much   35

for t'other, it there is demonstration of my friendship.
Ay, it must be so. I find I'm very much her friend.—Yet, let
me ask myself one puzzling question more. Whence springs
this mighty friendship all at once? For our acquaintance is
of later date. Now friendship's said to be a plant of tedious   40
growth; its root composed of tender fibres, nice in their
taste, cautious in spreading, checked with the last corruption
in the soil; long ere it take, and longer still ere it appear to do
so: whilst mine is in a moment shot so high, and fix'd so fast,
it seems beyond the power of storms to shake it. I doubt   45
it thrives too fast.   (*Musing*)

Enter BERINTHIA

Ha! she here!—Nay, then take heed, my heart, for there
are dangers towards.
BERINTHIA
What makes you look so thoughtful, sir? I hope you are not
ill.   50
LOVELESS
I was debating, madam, whether I was so or not; and that
was it which made me look so thoughtful.
BERINTHIA
Is it then so hard a matter to decide? I thought all people
had been acquainted with their own bodies, though few
people know their own minds.   55
LOVELESS
What if the distemper, I suspect, be in the mind?
BERINTHIA
Why, then I'll undertake to prescribe you a cure.
LOVELESS
Alas! you undertake you know not what.
BERINTHIA
So far at least then allow me to be a physician.
LOVELESS
Nay, I'll allow you so yet farther: for I have reason to   60
believe, should I put myself into your hands, you would
increase my distemper.
BERINTHIA
Perhaps I might have reasons from the College not to be too
quick in your cure; but 'tis possible I might find ways to give
you often ease, sir.   65

36 *it there is* (CE) If there is (Q1)
63 *College* the College of Physicians

LOVELESS
  Were I but sure of that, I'd quickly lay my case before you.
BERINTHIA
  Whether you are sure of it or no, what risk do you run in
  trying?
LOVELESS
  Oh! a very great one.
BERINTHIA
  How?   70
LOVELESS
  You might betray my distemper to my wife.
BERINTHIA
  And so lose all my practice.
LOVELESS
  Will you then keep my secret?
BERINTHIA
  I will, if it don't burst me.
LOVELESS
  Swear.   75
BERINTHIA
  I do.
LOVELESS
  By what?
BERINTHIA
  By Woman.
LOVELESS
  That's swearing by my deity. Do it by your own, or I shan't
  believe you.   80
BERINTHIA
  By Man, then.
LOVELESS
  I'm satisfied. Now hear my symptoms, and give me your
  advice.
  The first were these:
  When 'twas my chance to see you at the play,   85
  A random glance you threw at first alarmed me,
  I could not turn my eyes from whence the danger came.
  I gazed upon you till you shot again,
  And then my fears came on me.
  My heart began to pant, my limbs to tremble,   90
  My blood grew thin, my pulse beat quick, my eyes
  Grew hot and dim, and all the frame of nature

67 *Whether* (CE) whither (Q1)

Shook with apprehension.
'Tis true, some small recruits of resolution
My manhood brought to my assistance;   95
And by their help I made a stand awhile,
But found at last your arrows flew so thick,
They could not fail to pierce me; so left the field,
And fled for shelter to Amanda's arms.
What think you of these symptoms, pray?   100

BERINTHIA

Feverish, every one of 'em.
But what relief, pray, did your wife afford you?

LOVELESS

Why, instantly, she let me blood;
Which for the present much assuaged my flame.
But when I saw you, out it burst again,   105
And raged with greater fury than before.
Nay, since you now appear, 'tis so increased,
That in a moment, if you do not help me,
I shall, whilst you look on, consume to ashes.
                    (*Taking hold of her hand*)

BERINTHIA (*Breaking from him*)

O Lard, let me go! 'Tis the plague, and we shall all be   110
infected.

LOVELESS (*Catching her in his arms, and kissing her*)

Then we'll die together, my charming angel!

BERINTHIA

O Ged—the devil's in you!—Lord, let me go, here's somebody coming.

                    Enter SERVANT

SERVANT

Sir, my lady's come home, and desires to speak with you.   115
She's in her chamber.

LOVELESS

Tell her I'm coming.—(*Exit* SERVANT)
(*To* BERINTHIA) But before I go, one glass of nectar more
to drink her health.

BERINTHIA

Stand off, or I shall hate you, by Heavens!   120

LOVELESS (*Kissing her*)

In matters of love, a woman's oath is no more to be minded
than a man's.

BERINTHIA

Um—

                    Enter WORTHY

WORTHY (*Aside*)

Ha! what's here? My old mistress, and so close, i'faith! I
would not spoil her sport for the universe.   (*He retires*)   125

BERINTHIA

O Ged!—Now do I pray to heaven,—(*Exit* LOVELESS
running) with all my heart and soul, that the devil in hell
may take me—if ever—I was better pleased in my life! This
man has bewitched me, that's certain.—(*Sighing*) Well, I
am condemned; but, thanks to heaven, I feel myself each   130
moment more and more prepared for my execution. Nay,
to that degree, I don't perceive I have the least fear of dying.
No, I find, let the executioner be but a man, and there's
nothing will suffer with more resolution than a woman. Well,
I never had but one intrigue yet—but I confess I long to   135
have another. Pray heaven it end as the first did though,
that we may both grow weary at a time; for 'tis a melancholy
thing for lovers to outlive one another.

Enter WORTHY

WORTHY (*Aside*)

This discovery's a lucky one; I hope to make a happy use
on't. That gentlewoman there is no fool; so I shall be able   140
to make her understand her interest.—(*To* BERINTHIA)
Your servant, madam; I need not ask you how you do, you
have got so good a colour.

BERINTHIA

No better than I used to have, I suppose?

WORTHY

A little more blood in your cheeks.   145

BERINTHIA

The weather's hot.

WORTHY

If it were not, a woman may have a colour.

BERINTHIA

What do you mean by that?

WORTHY

Nothing.

BERINTHIA

Why do you smile then?   150

WORTHY

Because the weather's hot.

BERINTHIA

You'll never leave roguing, I see that.

WORTHY (*Putting his finger to his nose*)
    You'll never leave—I see that.
BERINTHIA
    Well, I can't imagine what you drive at. Pray tell me what
    you mean?   155
WORTHY
    Do you tell me; it's the same thing.
BERINTHIA
    I can't.
WORTHY
    Guess!
BERINTHIA
    I shall guess wrong.
WORTHY
    Indeed you won't.   160
BERINTHIA
    Psha! either tell, or let it alone.
WORTHY
    Nay, rather than let it alone, I will tell. But first I must put
    you in mind, that after what has passed 'twixt you and I, very
    few things ought to be secrets between us.
BERINTHIA
    Why, what secrets do we hide? I know of none.   165
WORTHY
    Yes, there are two; one I have hid from you, and t'other you
    would hide from me. You are fond of Loveless, which I have
    discovered; and I am fond of his wife—
BERINTHIA
    Which I have discovered.
WORTHY
    Very well, now I confess your discovery to be true: what   170
    do you say to mine?
BERINTHIA
    Why, I confess—I would swear 'twere false, if I thought
    you were fool enough to believe me.
WORTHY
    Now am I almost in love with you again. Nay, I don't
    know but I might be quite so, had I made one short cam-   175
    paign with Amanda. Therefore, if you find 'twould tickle
    your vanity to bring me down once more to your lure, e'en

156 Do you tell me its the same thing? (Q1)

help me quickly to dispatch her business, that I may have
nothing else to do, but to apply myself to yours.

BERINTHIA

Do you then think, sir, I am old enough to be a bawd?   180

WORTHY

No, but I think you are wise enough to—

BERINTHIA

To do what?

WORTHY

To hoodwink Amanda with a gallant, that she mayn't see
who is her husband's mistress.

BERINTHIA (*Aside*)

He has reason.—The hint's a good one.   185

WORTHY

Well, madam, what think you on't.

BERINTHIA

I think you are so much a deeper politician in these affairs
than I am, that I ought to have a very great regard to your
advice.

WORTHY

Then give me leave to put you in mind, that the most easy,   190
safe, and pleasant situation for your own amour, is the
house in which you now are; provided you keep Amanda
from any sort of suspicion. That the way to do that, is to
engage her in an intrigue of her own, making yourself her
confidante. And the way to bring her to intrigue, is to make 195
her jealous of her husband in a wrong place; which the
more you foment, the less you'll be suspected. This is my
scheme, in short; which if you follow as you should do, my
dear Berinthia, we may all four pass the winter very
pleasantly.   200

BERINTHIA

Well, I could be glad to have nobody's sins to answer for
but my own. But where there is a necessity—

WORTHY

Right as you say, where there is a necessity, a Christian is
bound to help his neighbour. So, good Berinthia, lose no
time, but let us begin the dance as fast as we can.   205

BERINTHIA

Not till the fiddles are in tune, pray, sir. Your lady's strings
will be very apt to fly, I can tell you that, if they are wound
up too hastily. But if you'll have patience to screw 'em to
their pitch by degrees, I don't doubt but she may endure to
be played upon.   210

WORTHY

Ay, and will make admirable music too, or I'm mistaken. But have you had no private closet discourse with her yet about males and females, and so forth, which may give you hopes in her constitution, for I know her morals are the devil against us?   215

BERINTHIA

I have had so much discourse with her, that I believe, were she once cured of her fondness to her husband, the fortress of her virtue would not be so impregnable as she fancies.

WORTHY

What! she runs, I'll warrant you, into that common mistake of fond wives, who conclude themselves virtuous because   220 they can refuse a man they don't like, when they have got one they do.

BERINTHIA

True; and therefore I think 'tis a presumptuous thing in a woman to assume the name of virtuous, till she has heartily hated her husband, and been soundly in love with somebody   225 else: whom, if she has withstood,—then—much good may it do her.

WORTHY

Well, so much for her virtue. Now, one word of her inclinations, and every one to their post. What opinion do you find she has of me?   230

BERINTHIA

What you could wish; she thinks you handsome and discreet.

WORTHY

Good; that's thinking half-seas over. One tide more brings us into port.

BERINTHIA

Perhaps it may, though still remember, there's a difficult bar to pass.   235

WORTHY

I know there is, but I don't question I shall get well over it, by the help of such a pilot.

BERINTHIA

You may depend upon your pilot, she'll do the best she can; so weigh anchor and begone as soon as you please.

WORTHY

I'm under sail already. Adieu!   (*Exit* WORTHY)   240

232 *thinking half-seas over* half-way there in thought

BERINTHIA

Bon voyage!

(*Sola*) So, here's fine work! What a business have I undertaken! I'm a very pretty gentlewoman truly! But there was
no avoiding it; he'd have ruined me, if I had refused him.
Besides, faith, I begin to fancy there may be as much   245
pleasure in carrying on another body's intrigues as one's
own. This at least is certain, it exercises almost all the
entertaining faculties of a woman; for there's employment
for hypocrisy, invention, deceit, flattery, mischief, and
lying.   250

Enter AMANDA, *her* WOMAN *following her*

WOMAN

If you please, madam, only to say whether you'll have me
buy 'em or not.

AMANDA

Yes, no, go fiddle! I care not what you do. Prithee leave me.

WOMAN

I have done.   (*Exit*)

BERINTHIA

What in the name of Jove's the matter with you?   255

AMANDA

The matter, Berinthia! I'm almost mad, I'm plagued to
death.

BERINTHIA

Who is it that plagues you?

AMANDA

Who do you think should plague a wife, but her husband?

BERINTHIA

O ho, is it come to that? We shall have you wish yourself a   260
widow by and by.

AMANDA

Would I were anything but what I am! A base, ungrateful
man, after what I have done for him, to use me thus!

BERINTHIA

What, he has been ogling now, I'll warrant you!

AMANDA

Yes, he has been ogling.   265

BERINTHIA

And so you are jealous? Is that all?

241 *Bon voyage!* The laboured exchange which this derisive remark
   completes is so overt that what might otherwise be the antithesis
   of wit becomes, in the theatre, an acceptable form of humour.

AMANDA

That all! Is jealousy then nothing?

BERINTHIA

It should be nothing, if I were in your case.

AMANDA

Why, what would you do?

BERINTHIA

I'd cure myself.   270

AMANDA

How?

BERINTHIA

Let blood in the fond vein: care as little for my husband as
he did for me.

AMANDA

That would not stop his course.

BERINTHIA

Nor nothing else, when the wind's in the warm corner. Look   275
you, Amanda, you may build castles in the air, and fume,
and fret, and grow thin and lean, and pale and ugly, if you
please. But I tell you, no man worth having is true to his
wife, or ever was, or ever will be so.

AMANDA

Do you then really think he's false to me? For I did but   280
suspect him.

BERINTHIA

Think so? I know he's so.

AMANDA

Is it possible? Pray tell me what you know.

BERINTHIA

Don't press me then to name names, for that I have sworn I
won't do.   285

AMANDA

Well, I won't; but let me know all you can without perjury.

BERINTHIA

I'll let you know enough to prevent any wise woman's dying
of the pip; and I hope you'll pluck up your spirits, and show
upon occasion you can be as good a wife as the best of 'em.

AMANDA

Well, what a woman can do I'll endeavour.   290

BERINTHIA

Oh, a woman can do a great deal, if once she sets her mind to
it. Therefore pray don't stand trifling any longer, and
teasing yourself with this and that, and your love and your
virtue, and I know not what: but resolve to hold up your

head, get a tip-toe, and look over 'em all; for to my certain   295
knowledge your husband is a-pickeering elsewhere.

AMANDA

You are sure on't?

BERINTHIA

Positively; he fell in love at the play.

AMANDA

Right, the very same. Do you know the ugly thing?

BERINTHIA

Yes, I know her well enough; but she's no such an ugly   300
thing neither.

AMANDA

Is she very handsome?

BERINTHIA

Truly I think so.

AMANDA

Hey ho!

BERINTHIA

What do you sigh for now?   305

AMANDA

Oh, my heart!

BERINTHIA (*Aside*)

Only the pangs of nature; she's in labour of her love; heaven
send her a quick delivery, I'm sure she has a good midwife.

AMANDA

I'm very ill, I must go to my chamber. Dear Berinthia, don't
leave me a moment.   310

BERINTHIA

No, don't fear.—(*Aside*) I'll see you safe brought to bed, I'll
warrant you.

(*Exeunt*, AMANDA *leaning upon* BERINTHIA)

Act III, Scene iii

A Country House
Enter YOUNG FASHION *and* LORY

FASHION

So, here's our inheritance, Lory, if we can but get into
possession. But methinks the seat of our family looks like
Noah's ark, as if the chief part on't were designed for the
fowls of the air, and the beasts of the field.

296 *a-pickeering* to pickeer is to reconnoitre, skirmish, or scout; hence,
like many military terms, adaptable to amorous meaning

4 * *

LORY

    Pray, sir, don't let your head run upon the orders of building   5
here; get but the heiress, let the devil take the house.

FASHION

    Get but the house, let the devil take the heiress, I say; at least
if she be as old Coupler describes her. But come, we have no
time to squander. Knock at the door.—(LORY *knocks two or*
three times) What the devil, have they got no ears in this   10
house? Knock harder.

LORY

    Egad, sir, this will prove some enchanted castle; we shall
have the giant come out by and by with his club, and beat
our brains out.   (*Knocks again*)

FASHION

    Hush! they come.   15

(*From within*) Who is there?

LORY

    Open the door and see. Is that your country breeding?

(*Within*)

    Ay, but two words to a bargain.—Tummas, is the blunder-
buss primed?

FASHION

    Oons, give 'em good words, Lory; we shall be shot here a   20
fortune-catching.

LORY

    Egad, sir, I think y'are in the right on't.—Ho! Mr
What-d'ye-call-um.

        (SERVANT *appears at the window with a blunderbuss*)

SERVANT

    Weall, naw what's yare business?

FASHION

    Nothing, sir, but to wait upon Sir Tunbelly, with your leave.   25

SERVANT

    To weat upon Sir Tunbelly? Why, you'll find that's just as
Sir Tunbelly pleases.

FASHION

    But will you do me the favour, sir, to know whether Sir
Tunbelly pleases or not?

---

  5 *orders of building* the classical orders of architecture, Doric, Ionic,
    and Corinthian: Vanbrugh's most notorious disrespect for the
    orders lay in contrasting Doric and Corinthian on the north and
    south fronts at Castle Howard, since both aspects could not
    be seen at the same time.

SERVANT

Why, look you, do you see, with good words much may be   30
done.—Ralph, go thy weas, and ask Sir Tunbelly if he
pleases to be waited upon. And dost hear? Call to nurse that
she may lock up Miss Hoyden before the geat's open.

FASHION

D'ye hear that, Lory?

LORY

Ay, sir, I'm afraid we shall find a difficult job on't. Pray   35
heaven that old rogue Coupler hasn't sent us to fetch milk
out of the gunroom.

FASHION

I'll warrant thee all will go well. See, the door opens.
Enter SIR TUNBELLY, *with his* SERVANTS *armed with guns, clubs,
pitchforks, scythes, &c.*

LORY (*Running behind his master*)

O Lord! O Lord! O Lord! We are both dead men!

FASHION

Take heed, fool! Thy fear will ruin us.   40

LORY

My fear, sir! 'Sdeath, sir, I fear nothing.—(*Aside*) Would I
were well up to the chin in a horsepond!

SIR TUNBELLY

Who is it here has any business with me?

FASHION

Sir, 'tis I, if your name be Sir Tunbelly Clumsey.

SIR TUNBELLY

Sir, my name is Sir Tunbelly Clumsey, whether you have   45
any business with me or not. So you see I am not ashamed
of my name—nor my face neither.

FASHION

Sir, you have no cause, that I know of.

SIR TUNBELLY

Sir, if you have no cause neither, I desire to know who you
are; for till I know your name, I shall not ask you to come   50
into my house; and when I know your name—'tis six to
four I don't ask you neither.

FASHION (*Giving him a letter*)

Sir, I hope you'll find this letter an authentic passport.

SIR TUNBELLY

Cod's my life! I ask your lordship's pardon ten thousand

36-7 *to fetch . . . gunroom* Lory's remark is credited by O.E.D. (under
    'Gunroom') as proverbial.
45 *whether* (CE) whither (Q1)

times.—(*To a* SERVANT) Here, run in a-doors quickly. Get a   55
Scotch-coal fire in the great parlour; set all the Turkey-work
chairs in their places; get the great brass candlesticks out,
and be sure stick the sockets full of laurel, run!—(*Turning
to* YOUNG FASHION) My lord, I ask your lordship's pardon.—
(*To other* SERVANTS) And do you hear, run away to nurse,   60
bid her let Miss Hoyden loose again, and if it was not
shifting day, let her put on a clean tucker, quick!—(*Exeunt
SERVANTS confusedly*). (*To* YOUNG FASHION) I hope your
honour will excuse the disorder of my family; we are not used
to receive men of your lordship's great quality every day.   65
Pray where are your coaches and servants, my lord?

FASHION

Sir, that I might give you and your fair daughter a proof how
impatient I am to be nearer akin to you, I left my equipage
to follow me, and came away post with only one servant.

SIR TUNBELLY

Your lordship does me too much honour. It was exposing   70
your person to too much fatigue and danger, I protest it was.
But my daughter shall endeavour to make you what amends
she can; and though I say it that should not say it—Hoyden
has charms.

FASHION

Sir, I am not a stranger to them, though I am to her.   75
Common fame has done her justice.

SIR TUNBELLY

My lord, I am common fame's very grateful humble servant.
My lord—my girl's young, Hoyden is young, my lord; but
this I must say for her, what she wants in art, she has by
nature; what she wants in experience, she has in breeding;   80
and what's wanting in her age, is made good in her constitution. So pray, my lord, walk in: pray, my lord, walk in.

FASHION

Sir, I wait upon you.   (*Exeunt*)

55–8 *Get a . . . run!* We may assume that Sir Tunbelly is doing his
  best to make amends and that Vanbrugh is, unironically, allowing
  him the superlatives of provincial living; but *Scotch-coal* is so
  little known that O.E.D. attributes the phrase to Sheridan's *A
  Trip to Scarborough*—perhaps it is simply rarer than Newcastle
  coal; *Turkey-work* means a design in imitation of Turkish
  tapestry; and to decorate the candle sockets with laurel is probably to revive a Christmas custom of festivity.
62 *shifting day* day for a fresh change of shift *tucker* chemise

Act III, Scene iv

MISS HOYDEN *sola*

HOYDEN

Sure, never nobody was used as I am. I know well enough
what other girls do, for all they think to make a fool of me.
It's well I have a husband a-coming, or, ecod, I'd marry
the baker, I would so! Nobody can knock at the gate, but
presently I must be locked up; and here's the young grey-   5
hound bitch can run loose about the house all day long,
she can; 'tis very well.

NURSE (*Without; opening the door*)

Miss Hoyden! miss! miss! miss! Miss Hoyden!

Enter NURSE

HOYDEN

Well, what do you make such a noise for, ha? What do you
din a body's ears for? Can't one be at quiet for you?   10

NURSE

What do I din your ears for? Here's one come will din your
ears for you.

HOYDEN

What care I who's come? I care not a fig who comes, nor
who goes, as long as I must be locked up like the ale-cellar.

NURSE

That, miss, is for fear you should be drank before you are   15
ripe.

HOYDEN

Oh, don't trouble your head about that; I'm ripe as you,
though not so mellow.

NURSE

Very well; now have I a good mind to lock you up again, and
not let you see my lord tonight.   20

HOYDEN

My lord? Why, is my husband come?

NURSE

Yes, marry is he, and a goodly person, too.

HOYDEN (*Hugging* NURSE)

O my dear nurse! forgive me this once, and I'll never mis-
use you again; no, if I do, you shall give me three thumps on
the back, and a great pinch by the cheek.   25

8 s.d. This establishes that the scene takes place in a room in Sir
    Tunbelly Clumsey's house.
8 The Q1 prefix 'MISS' has been changed to 'HOYDEN' throughout.

NURSE

Ah, the poor thing, see how it melts. It's as full of good-nature as an egg's full of meat.

HOYDEN

But, my dear nurse, don't lie now; is he come by your troth?

NURSE

Yes, by my truly, is he.

HOYDEN

O Lord! I'll go put on my laced smock, though I'm whipped   30
till the blood run down my heels for't.   (*Exit running*)

NURSE

Eh—the Lord succour thee! How thou art delighted.

(*Exit after her*)

Act III, Scene v

Enter SIR TUNBELLY *and* YOUNG FASHION
a SERVANT *with wine*

SIR TUNBELLY

My lord, I am proud of the honour to see your lordship within my doors; and I humbly crave leave to bid you welcome in a cup of sack wine.

FASHION

Sir, to your daughter's health.   (*Drinks*)

SIR TUNBELLY

Ah, poor girl, she'll be scared out of her wits on her wedding-   5
night; for, honestly speaking, she does not know a man from a woman but by his beard and his breeches.

FASHION

Sir, I don't doubt but she has a virtuous education, which with the rest of her merit makes me long to see her mine; I wish you would dispense with the canonical hour, and let   10
it be this very night.

SIR TUNBELLY

Oh, not so soon neither! that's shooting my girl before you bid her stand. No, give her fair warning, we'll sign and seal tonight, if you please; and this day sevennight—let the jade look to her quarters.   15

FASHION

This day sennight!—why, what do you take me for, a ghost, sir? 'Slife, sir, I'm made of flesh and blood, and bones and

2 *within my doors* again presumably a room in Sir Tunbelly's house.

sinews, and can no more live a week without your daughter—
(*Aside*) than I can live a month with her.

SIR TUNBELLY

Oh, I'll warrant you, my hero; young men are hot, I know,   20
but they don't boil over at that rate, neither. Besides, my
wench's wedding-gown is not come home yet.

FASHION

Oh, no matter, sir, I'll take her in her shift.—(*Aside*) A pox
of this old fellow! he'll delay the business till my damned
star finds me out and discovers me.—(*To* SIR TUNBELLY)   25
Pray, sir, let it be done without ceremony, 'twill save money.

SIR TUNBELLY

Money?—Save money when Hoyden's to be married?
Udswoons, I'll give my wench a wedding-dinner, though
I go to grass with the King of Assyria for't; and such a
dinner it shall be, as is not to be cooked in the poaching of an   30
egg. Therefore, my noble lord, have a little patience, we'll go
and look over our deeds and settlements immediately;
and as for your bride, though you may be sharp-set before
she's quite ready, I'll engage for my girl, she stays your
stomach at last.   (*Exeunt*)   35

Act IV, Scene i

Enter MISS HOYDEN *and* NURSE

NURSE

Well, miss, how do you like your husband that is to be?

HOYDEN

O Lord, nurse, I'm so overjoyed I can scarce contain myself.

NURSE

Oh, but you must have a care of being too fond; for men
now-a-days hate a woman that loves 'em.

HOYDEN

Love him? Why, do you think I love him, nurse? Ecod, I   5
would not care if he were hanged, so I were but once married
to him.—No—that which please me, is to think what work

---

29 *King of Assyria* Sir Tunbelly is undoubtedly thinking of Nebu-
  chadnezzar, King of Babylon, but Vanbrugh could not resist the
  more fitting title.
35 s.d. (*Exeunt*) Q1 follows this with 'End of the Third Act'.
 1 Presumably this conversation takes place in the same location
  as III, iv.

I'll make when I get to London; for when I am a wife and a
lady both, nurse, ecod, I'll flaunt it with the best of 'em.

NURSE

Look, look, if his honour be not coming again to you. Now,   10
if I were sure you would behave yourself handsomely, and not
disgrace me that have brought you up, I'd leave you alone
together.

HOYDEN

That's my best nurse, do as you would be done by: trust us
together this once, and if I don't show my breeding from the   15
head to the foot of me, may I be twice married, and die a
maid.

NURSE

Well, this once I'll venture you; but if you disparage me—

HOYDEN

Never fear, I'll show him my parts, I'll warrant him.
                    (*Exit* NURSE. *Sola*)
These old women are so wise when they get a poor girl in   20
their clutches! but ere it be long, I shall know what's what,
as well as the best of 'em.

Enter YOUNG FASHION

FASHION

Your servant, madam; I'm glad to find you alone, for I have
something of importance to speak to you about.

HOYDEN

Sir (my lord, I meant), you may speak to me about what   25
you please, I shall give you a civil answer.

FASHION

You give me so obliging a one, it encourages me to tell you
in few words what I think both for your interest and mine.
Your father, I suppose you know, has resolved to make me
happy in being your husband, and I hope I may depend   30
upon your consent, to perform what he desires.

HOYDEN

Sir, I never disobey my father in anything, but eating of
green gooseberries.

FASHION

So good a daughter must needs make an admirable wife; I am
therefore impatient till you are mine, and hope you will so   35
far consider the violence of my love, that you won't have the

9 *flaunt* flant (Q1)

cruelty to defer my happiness so long as your father designs
it.

HOYDEN

Pray, my lord, how long is that?

FASHION

Madam, a thousand year—a whole week.   40

HOYDEN

A week!—Why, I shall be an old woman by that time.

FASHION

And I an old man, which you'll find a greater misfortune
than t'other.

HOYDEN

Why, I thought 'twas to be tomorrow morning, as soon as
I was up; I'm sure nurse told me so.   45

FASHION

And it shall be tomorrow morning still, if you'll consent?

HOYDEN

If I'll consent? Why, I thought I was to obey you as my
husband?

FASHION

That's when we are married; till then I am to obey you.

HOYDEN

Why then, if we are to take it by turns, it's the same thing.   50
I'll obey you now; and when we are married, you shall obey
me.

FASHION

With all my heart; but I doubt we must get nurse on our
side, or we shall hardly prevail with the chaplain.

HOYDEN

No more we shan't indeed, for he loves her better than he   55
loves his pulpit, and would always be a-preaching to her
by his good will.

FASHION

Why then, my dear little bedfellow, if you'll call her hither,
we'll try to persuade her presently.

HOYDEN

O Lord, I can tell you a way how to persuade her to anything.   60

FASHION

How's that?

HOYDEN

Why, tell her she's a wholesome comely woman—and give
her half-a-crown.

FASHION

Nay, if that will do, she shall have half a score of 'em.

HOYDEN

O Gemini! for half that she'd marry you herself. I'll run and   65
call her.   (*Exit*)

FASHION (*Solus*)

So, matters go swimmingly. This is a rare girl, i'faith; I shall
have a fine time on't with her at London. I'm much mistaken
if she don't prove a March hare all the year round. What a
scampering chase will she make on't, when she finds the   70
whole kennel of beaux at her tail! Hey to the park, and the
play, and the church, and the devil; she'll show 'em sport,
I'll warrant 'em. But no matter, she brings an estate will
afford me a separate maintenance.

Enter MISS HOYDEN *and* NURSE

How do you do, good mistress nurse? I desired your young   75
lady would give me leave to see you, that I might thank you
for your extraordinary care and conduct in her education;
pray accept of this small acknowledgment for it at present,
and depend upon my farther kindness, when I shall be that
happy thing her husband.   80

NURSE (*Aside*)

Gold, by makings!—[*Aloud*] Your honour's goodness is too
great; alas! all I can boast of is, I gave her pure good milk,
and so your honour would have said, an you had seen how
the poor thing sucked it.—Eh, God's blessing on the sweet
face on't! how it used to hang at this poor teat, and suck and   85
squeeze, and kick and sprawl it would, till the belly on't was
so full, it would drop off like a leech.

HOYDEN (*To* NURSE, *taking her angrily aside*)

Pray one word with you. Prithee nurse, don't stand ripping
up old stories, to make one ashamed before one's love. Do
you think such a fine proper gentleman as he cares for a   90
fiddlecome tale of a draggle-tailed girl? If you have a mind
to make him have a good opinion of a woman, don't tell him
what one did then, tell him what one can do now.—(*To*
YOUNG FASHION) I hope your honour will excuse my mis-
manners to whisper before you; it was only to give some   95
orders about the family.

---

65 *Gemini* one of the commonest of trivial expletives of the time; it
  has nothing to do with the heavenly twins, but is a prior form of
  'jiminy', Low Dutch in origin and probably pseudo-blasphemous
  ('jesu domine').

81 *makings* the basis from which something further may be made

FASHION

Oh everything, madam, is to give way to business. Besides, good housewifery is a very commendable quality in a young lady.

HOYDEN

Pray, sir, are the young ladies good housewives at London 100
town? Do they darn their own linen?

FASHION

Oh no, they study how to spend money, not to save it.

HOYDEN

Ecod, I don't know but that may be better sport than t'other; ha, nurse?

FASHION

Well, you shall have your choice when you come there.   105

HOYDEN

Shall I?—then by my troth I'll get there as fast as I can.
—(*To* NURSE) His honour desires you'll be so kind as to let us
be married tomorrow.

NURSE

Tomorrow, my dear madam?

FASHION

Yes, tomorrow, sweet nurse, privately; young folks, you 110
know, are impatient, and Sir Tunbelly would make us stay
a week for a wedding dinner. Now all things being signed
and sealed and agreed, I fancy there could be no great harm
in practising a scene or two of matrimony in private, if it were
only to give us the better assurance when we come to play 115
it in public.

NURSE

Nay, I must confess stolen pleasures are sweet; but if you
should be married now, what will you do when Sir Tunbelly
calls for you to be wed?

HOYDEN

Why then we'll be married again.   120

NURSE

What, twice, my child?

HOYDEN

Ecod, I don't care how often I'm married, not I.

FASHION

Pray, nurse, don't you be against your young lady's good,
for by this means she'll have the pleasure of two wedding-
days.   125

HOYDEN (*To* NURSE *softly*)

And of two wedding-nights, too, nurse.

NURSE

Well, I'm such a tender-hearted fool, I find I can refuse
nothing; so you shall e'en follow your own inventions.

HOYDEN

Shall I?—(*Aside*) O Lord, I could leap over the moon!

FASHION

Dear nurse, this goodness of yours shan't go unrewarded;   130
but now you must employ your power with Mr Bull the
chaplain, that he may do us his friendly office too, and then
we shall all be happy. Do you think you can prevail with
him?

NURSE

Prevail with him?—or he shall never prevail with me, I can   135
tell him that.

HOYDEN

My lord, she has had him upon the hip this seven year.

FASHION

I'm glad to hear it; however, to strengthen your interest with
him, you may let him know I have several fat livings in my
gift, and that the first that falls shall be in your disposal.   140

NURSE

Nay, then I'll make him marry more folks than one, I'll
promise him.

HOYDEN

Faith do, nurse, make him marry you too, I'm sure he'll do't
for a fat living; for he loves eating more than he loves his
Bible; and I have often heard him say, a fat living was the   145
best meat in the world.

NURSE

Ay, and I'll make him commend the sauce, too, or I'll bring
his gown to a cassock, I will so.

FASHION

Well, nurse, whilst you go and settle matters with him,
then your lady and I will go take a walk in the garden.   150

NURSE

I'll do your honour's business in the catching up of a
garter.   (*Exit*)

137 *upon the hip* an obvious pun upon the wrestling term, implying
     both pleasure and advantage
147–8 *bring . . . cassock* Nurse expresses her confidence in her hold
     over the chaplain by reverting to an ancient quarrel within the
     church, involving celibacy; if Bull will not provide sauce for the
     goose he may not have much future as a gander.

FASHION (*Giving her his hand*)

Come, madam, dare you venture yourself alone with me?

HOYDEN

O dear, yes, sir, I don't think you'll do anything to me I need
be afraid on.   (*Exeunt*)   155

Act IV, Scene ii

Enter AMANDA *and* BERINTHIA

A Song

I

I smile at Love and all its arts,
   The charming Cynthia cried:
Take heed, for Love has piercing darts,
   A wounded swain replied.
Once free and blest as you are now,   5
   I trifled with his charms,
I pointed at his little bow,
   And sported with his arms:
Till urged too far, Revenge! he cries,
   A fatal shaft he drew,   10
It took its passage through your eyes,
   And to my heart it flew.

II

To tear it thence I tried in vain,
   To strive, I quickly found,
Was only to increase the pain,   15
   And to enlarge the wound.
Ah! much too well, I fear, you know
   What pain I'm to endure,
Since what your eyes alone could do,
   Your heart alone can cure.   20
And that (grant heaven I may mistake)
   I doubt is doomed to bear
A burden for another's sake,
   Who ill rewards its care.

AMANDA

Well, now, Berinthia, I'm at leisure to hear what 'twas you   25
had to say to me.

BERINTHIA

What I had to say was only to echo the sighs and groans of a
dying lover.

1 *I smile* The scene has changed to Loveless's lodgings.

AMANDA

Phu! will you never learn to talk in earnest of anything?

BERINTHIA

Why this shall be in earnest, if you please. For my part, I only   30
tell you matter of fact, you may take it which way you like
best; but if you'll follow the women of the town, you'll take
it both ways; for when a man offers himself to one of them,
first she takes him in jest, and then she takes him in earnest.

AMANDA

I'm sure there's so much jest and earnest in what you say to   35
me, I scarce know how to take it; but I think you have
bewitched me, for I don't find it possible to be angry with
you, say what you will.

BERINTHIA

I'm very glad to hear it, for I have no mind to quarrel with
you, for more reasons than I'll brag of; but quarrel or not,   40
smile or frown, I must tell you what I have suffered upon
your account.

AMANDA

Upon my account?

BERINTHIA

Yes, upon yours; I have been forced to sit still and hear you
commended for two hours together, without one compliment   45
to myself; now don't you think a woman had a blessed time
of that?

AMANDA

Alas! I should have been unconcerned at it; I never knew
where the pleasure lay of being praised by the men. But pray
who was this that commended me so?   50

BERINTHIA

One you have a mortal aversion to, Mr Worthy; he used you
like a text, he took you all to pieces, but spoke so learnedly
upon every point, one might see the spirit of the church was
in him. If you are a woman, you'd have been in an ecstacy
to have heard how feelingly he handled your hair, your eyes,   55
your nose, your mouth, your teeth, your tongue, your chin,
your neck, and so forth. Thus he preached for an hour, but
when he came to use an application, he observed that all these
without a gallant were nothing. Now consider of what has
been said, and heaven give you grace to put it in practice.   60

AMANDA

Alas! Berinthia, did I incline to a gallant (which you know

43 AMANDA *Upon my account?* (CE) BERINTHIA *Upon my account?* (Q1)

I do not), do you think a man so nice as he could have the
least concern for such a plain unpolished thing as I am? It is
impossible!

BERINTHIA

Now have you a great mind to put me upon commending   65
you.

AMANDA

Indeed that was not my design.

BERINTHIA

Nay, if it were, it's all one, for I won't do't; I'll leave that to
your looking-glass. But to show you I have some good nature
left, I'll commend him, and may be that may do as well.   70

AMANDA

You have a great mind to persuade me I am in love with him.

BERINTHIA

I have a great mind to persuade you, you don't know what
you are in love with.

AMANDA

I am sure I am not in love with him, nor never shall be, so
let that pass. But you were saying something you would   75
commend him for.

BERINTHIA

Oh, you'd be glad to hear a good character of him, however.

AMANDA

Psha!

BERINTHIA

Psha!—Well, 'tis a foolish undertaking for women in these
kind of matters to pretend to deceive one another.—Have not   80
I been bred a woman as well as you?

AMANDA

What then?

BERINTHIA

Why, then I understand my trade so well, that whenever I
am told of a man I like, I cry, Psha! But that I may spare
you the pains of putting me a second time in mind to com-   85
mend him, I'll proceed, and give you this account of him.
That though 'tis possible he may have had women with as
good faces as your ladyship's, (no discredit to it neither), yet
you must know your cautious behaviour, with that reserve in
your humour, has given him his death's wound. He mortally   90
hates a coquette. He says 'tis impossible to love where we
cannot esteem; and that no woman can be esteemed by a man
who has sense, if she makes herself cheap in the eye of a fool.
That pride to a woman is as necessary as humility to a divine;

and that far-fetched and dear-bought, is meat for gentlemen   95
as well as for ladies;—in short, that every woman who has
beauty may set a price upon herself, and that by under-selling
the market, they ruin the trade. This is his doctrine, how do
you like it?

AMANDA

So well, that since I never intend to have a gallant for myself,   100
if I were to recommend one to a friend, he should be the man.

Enter WORTHY

Bless me! he's here, pray heaven he did not hear me.

BERINTHIA

If he did, it won't hurt your reputation; your thoughts are as
safe in his heart as in your own.

WORTHY

I venture in at an unseasonable time of night, ladies; I hope,   105
if I'm troublesome, you'll use the same freedom in turning
me out again.

AMANDA

I believe it can't be late, for Mr Loveless is not come home
yet, and he usually keeps good hours.

WORTHY

Madam, I'm afraid he'll transgress a little tonight; for he   110
told me about half an hour ago, he was going to sup with
some company he doubted would keep him out till three or
four o'clock in the morning, and desired I would let my
servant acquaint you with it, that you might not expect him:
but my fellow's a blunderhead; so lest he should make some   115
mistake, I thought it my duty to deliver the message myself.

AMANDA

I'm very sorry he should give you that trouble, sir: but—

BERINTHIA

But since he has, will you give me leave, madam, to keep him
to play at ombre with us?

AMANDA

Cousin, you know you command my house.   120

WORTHY (*To* BERINTHIA)

And, madam, you know you command me, though I'm a very
wretched gamester.

BERINTHIA

Oh, you play well enough to lose your money, and that's all

119 *ombre* a card game

the ladies require; so without any more ceremony, let us go
into the next room and call for the cards.   125

AMANDA

   With all my heart.   (*Exit* WORTHY, *leading* AMANDA)

BERINTHIA (*Sola*)

Well, how this business will end heaven knows; but she
seems to me to be in as fair a way—as a boy is to be a rogue,
when he's put clerk to an attorney.   (*Exit*)

Act IV, Scene iii

BERINTHIA's *Chamber*
Enter LOVELESS *cautiously in the dark*

LOVELESS

So, thus far all's well. I'm got into her bed-chamber, and I
think nobody has perceived me steal into the house; my wife
don't expect me home till four o'clock; so, if Berinthia comes
to bed by eleven, I shall have a chase of five hours. Let me
see, where shall I hide myself? Under her bed? No; we   5
shall have her maid searching there for something or other;
her closet's a better place, and I have a master-key will open
it. I'll e'en in there, and attack her just when she comes to her
prayers; that's the most likely to prove her critical minute, for
then the devil will be there to assist me.   10

   (*He opens the closet, goes in, and shuts the door after him*)

Enter BERINTHIA, *with a candle in her hand*

BERINTHIA

Well, sure, I am the best-natured woman in the world, I that
love cards so well (there is but one thing upon earth I love
better), have pretended letters to write, to give my friends
a *tête-à-tête*. However, I'm innocent, for picquet is the game
I set 'em to; at her own peril be it, if she ventures to play   15
with him at any other. But now what shall I do with myself?
I don't know how in the world to pass my time; would
Loveless were here to *badiner* a little! Well, he's a charming
fellow; I don't wonder his wife's so fond of him. What if I
should sit down and think of him till I fall asleep, and dream   20
of the Lord knows what? Oh, but then if I should dream we
were married, I should be frightened out of my wits!—
(*Seeing a book*) What's this book? I think I had best go read.
O splénétique, it's a sermon. Well, I'll go into my closet,

14 *tête-à-tête* à Tate à Tate (Q1)

and read *The Plotting Sisters.*—(*She opens the closet, sees*   25
LOVELESS, *and shrieks out*)
O Lord, a ghost! a ghost! a ghost! a ghost!

Enter LOVELESS, *running to her*

LOVELESS
Peace, my dear, it's no ghost; take it in your arms, you'll
find 'tis worth a hundred of 'em.
BERINTHIA
Run in again; here's somebody coming.

[LOVELESS *retires as before*]

Enter her MAID

MAID
Lord, madam! what's the matter?   30
BERINTHIA
O Heavens! I'm almost frightened out of my wits; I thought
verily I had seen a ghost, and 'twas nothing but the white
curtain, with a black hood pinned up against it: you may be
gone again; I am the fearfull'st fool!   (*Exit* MAID)

Re-enter LOVELESS

LOVELESS
Is the coast clear?   35
BERINTHIA
The coast clear! I suppose you are clear, you'd never play
such a trick as this else.
LOVELESS
I'm very well pleased with my trick thus far, and shall be so
till I have played it out, if it ben't your fault. Where's my
wife?   40
BERINTHIA
At cards.
LOVELESS
With whom?
BERINTHIA
With Worthy.
LOVELESS
Then we are safe enough.
BERINTHIA
Are you so? Some husbands would be of another mind, if   45
he were at cards with their wives.

---

25 *The Plotting Sisters* Thomas Durfey's *A Fond Husband, or The
   Plotting Sisters* (1677).
36 *you are clear* drunk, in the paradoxical sense of illuminated

LOVELESS

　And they'd be in the right on't, too: but I dare trust mine.—
　Besides, I know he's in love in another place, and he's not
　one of those who court half-a-dozen at a time.

BERINTHIA

　Nay, the truth on't is, you'd pity him if you saw how uneasy　50
　he is at being engaged with us; but 'twas my malice; I
　fancied he was to meet his mistress somewhere else, so did it
　to have the pleasure of seeing him fret.

LOVELESS

　What says Amanda to my staying abroad so late?

BERINTHIA

　Why, she's as much out of humour as he; I believe they wish　55
　one another at the devil.

LOVELESS

　Then I'm afraid they'll quarrel at play, and soon throw up
　the cards.—(*Offering to pull her into the closet*) Therefore, my
　dear, charming angel, let us make a good use of our time.

BERINTHIA

　Heavens! what do you mean?　　　　　　　　　　　　　　60

LOVELESS

　Pray what do you think I mean?

BERINTHIA

　I don't know.

LOVELESS

　I'll show you.

BERINTHIA

　You may as well tell me.

LOVELESS

　No, that would make you blush worse than t'other.　　　65

BERINTHIA

　Why, do you intend to make me blush?

LOVELESS

　Faith, I can't tell that; but if I do, it shall be in the dark.
　　　　　　　　　　　　　　　　　　　　　　(*Pulling her*)

BERINTHIA

　O Heavens! I would not be in the dark with you for all the
　world.

LOVELESS

　I'll try that.　　　　　　　　　　(*Puts out the candles*)　70

BERINTHIA

　O Lord! are you mad? What shall I do for light?

LOVELESS

　You'll do as well without it.

BERINTHIA

Why, one can't find a chair to sit down.

LOVELESS

Come into the closet, madam, there's moonshine upon the
couch.   75

BERINTHIA

Nay, never pull, for I will not go.

LOVELESS

Then you must be carried.   (*Carrying her*)

BERINTHIA (*Very softly*)

Help! help! I'm ravished! ruined! undone! O Lord, I shall
never be able to bear it. [*Exit* LOVELESS *carrying* BERINTHIA]

Act IV, Scene iv

SIR TUNBELLY's *House*
Enter MISS HOYDEN, NURSE, YOUNG FASHION, *and* BULL

FASHION

This quick dispatch of yours, Mr Bull, I take so kindly, it
shall give you a claim to my favour as long as I live, I do
assure you.

HOYDEN

And to mine, too, I promise you.

BULL

I most humbly thank your honours; and I hope, since it   5
has been my lot to join you in the holy bands of wedlock,
you will so cultivate the soil, which I have craved a blessing
on, that your children may swarm about you like bees about
a honeycomb.

HOYDEN

Ecod, with all my heart; the more the merrier, I say; ha,   10
nurse?

Enter LORY; *he takes his master hastily aside*

LORY

One word with you, for heaven's sake!

FASHION

What the devil's the matter?

LORY

Sir, your fortune's ruined; and I don't think your life's   15
worth a quarter of an hour's purchase. Yonder's your
brother arrived with two coaches and six horses, twenty foot-

men and pages, a coat worth four-score pound, and a periwig
down to his knees: so judge what will become of your lady's
heart.

FASHION

Death and furies! 'tis impossible! 20

LORY

Fiends and spectres! sir, 'tis true.

FASHION

Is he in the house yet?

LORY

No, they are capitulating with him at the gate. The porter
tells him he's come to run away with Miss Hoyden, and has
cocked the blunderbuss at him; your brother swears Gad 25
damme, they are a parcel of clawns, and he has a good mind to
break off the match; but they have given the word for Sir
Tunbelly, so I doubt all will come out presently. Pray, sir,
resolve what you'll do this moment, for egad they'll maul you.

FASHION

Stay a little.—(*To* MISS HOYDEN) My dear, here's a trouble- 30
some business my man tells me of, but don't be frightened,
we shall be too hard for the rogue. Here's an impudent
fellow at the gate (not knowing I was come hither *incognito*)
has taken my name upon him, in hopes to run away with you.

HOYDEN

Oh the brazen-faced varlet, it's well we are married, or maybe 35
we might never a been so.

FASHION (*Aside*)

Egad, like enough!—[*Aloud*] Prithee, dear doctor, run to
Sir Tunbelly, and stop him from going to the gate before I
speak with him.

BULL

I fly, my good lord. (*Exit*) 40

NURSE

An't please your honour, my lady and I had best lock our-
selves up till the danger be over.

FASHION

Ay, by all means.

HOYDEN

Not so fast, I won't be locked up any more. I'm married.

FASHION

Yes, pray, my dear, do, till we have seized this rascal. 45

---

23 *capitulating* Lory means negotiating, but anticipates defeat.

HOYDEN

Nay, if you pray me, I'll do anything.

(*Exeunt* MISS HOYDEN *and* NURSE)

FASHION

Oh! here's Sir Tunbelly coming. (*To* LORY) Hark you, sirrah, things are better than you imagine; the wedding's over.

LORY

The devil it is, sir!

FASHION

Not a word, all's safe; but Sir Tunbelly don't know it, nor   50
must not yet; so I am resolved to brazen the business out, and have the pleasure of turning the impostor upon his lordship, which I believe may easily be done.

Enter SIR TUNBELLY, CHAPLAIN, *and* SERVANTS *armed*

FASHION

Did you ever hear, sir, of so impudent an undertaking!

SIR TUNBELLY

Never, by the mass! But we'll tickle him, I'll warrant him.   55

FASHION

They tell me, sir, he has a great many people with him disguised like servants.

SIR TUNBELLY

Ay, ay, rogues enough; but I'll soon raise the posse upon 'em.

FASHION

Sir, if you'll take my advice, we'll go a shorter way to work. I find whoever this spark is, he knows nothing of my being   60
privately here; so if you pretend to receive him civilly, he'll enter without suspicion; and as soon as he is within the gate, we'll whip up the drawbridge upon his back, let fly the blunderbuss to disperse his crew, and so commit him to jail.

SIR TUNBELLY

Egad, your lordship is an ingenious person, and a very great   65
general; but shall we kill any of 'em or not?

FASHION

No, no; fire over their heads only to frighten 'em; I'll warrant the regiment scours when the colonel's a prisoner.

SIR TUNBELLY

Then come along, my boys, and let your courage be great—
for your danger is but small.   (*Exeunt*)   70

Act IV, Scene v

The Gate
Enter LORD FOPPINGTON *and* FOLLOWERS

LORD FOPPINGTON
A pax of these bumpkinly people! Will they open the gate, or
do they desire I should grow at their moat-side like a willow?
—(*To the* PORTER) Hey, fellow—prithee do me the favour, in
as few words as thou canst find to express thyself, to tell me
whether thy master will admit me or not, that I may turn   5
about my coach, and be gone.

PORTER
Here's my master himself now at hand; he's of age, he'll give
you his answer.

Enter SIR TUNBELLY *and* SERVANTS

SIR TUNBELLY
My most noble lord, I crave your pardon for making your
honour wait so long; but my orders to my servants have   10
been to admit nobody without my knowledge, for fear of,
some attempt upon my daughter, the times being full of
plots and roguery.

LORD FOPPINGTON
Much caution, I must confess, is a sign of great wisdom: but,
stap my vitals, I have got a cold enough to destroy a porter!   15
—He, hem—

SIR TUNBELLY
I am very sorry for't, indeed, my lord; but if your lordship
please to walk in, we'll help you to some brown sugar-candy.
My lord, I'll show you the way.

LORD FOPPINGTON
Sir, I follow you with pleasure.   20

[*Exit with* SIR TUNBELLY CLUMSEY]

(*As* LORD FOPPINGTON's SERVANTS *go to follow him in, they
clap the door against* LA VÉROLE)

SERVANTS (*Within*)
Nay, hold you me there, sir.

LA VÉROLE
Jernie die, qu'est-ce que veut dire ça?

SIR TUNBELLY (*Within*)
Fire, porter

22 *Jernie die* possibly a corruption of *Je renie dieu*

PORTER (*Fires*)

Have among ye, my masters.

LA VÉROLE

Ah, je suis mort!—   25

(*The* SERVANTS *all run off*)

PORTER

Not one soldier left, by the mass!

Act IV, Scene vi

[*The Hall*]

Enter SIR TUNBELLY, *the* CHAPLAIN *and* SERVANTS,
with LORD FOPPINGTON *disarmed*

SIR TUNBELLY

Come, bring him along, bring him along.

LORD FOPPINGTON

What the pax to you mean, gentlemen! Is it Fair-time, that
you are all drunk before dinner?

SIR TUNBELLY

Drunk, sirrah!—Here's an impudent rogue for you. Drunk or
sober, bully, I'm a Justice of the Peace, and know how to   5
deal with strollers.

LORD FOPPINGTON

Strollers!

SIR TUNBELLY

Ay, strollers. Come, give an account of yourself; what's
your name, where do you live? Do you pay scot and lot?
Are you a Williamite, or a Jacobite? Come.   10

LORD FOPPINGTON

And why dost thou ask me so many impertinent questions?

SIR TUNBELLY

Because I'll make you answer 'em before I have done with
you, you rascal you!

LORD FOPPINGTON

Before Gad, all the answer I can make thee to 'em is, that
thou art a very extraordinary old fellow, stap my vitals!   15

SIR TUNBELLY

Nay, if you are for joking with deputy lieutenants, we'st know

26 *by the mass*! Q1 follows this with '*Scene changes to the hall*'.
 6 *strollers* vagabonds
 9 *scot and lot* a parish assessment, determined by ability to pay
10 *Williamite . . . Jacobite* a supporter of King William III or of James
   II in exile

how to deal with you. Here, draw a warrant for him immediately.

LORD FOPPINGTON

A warrant! What the devil is't thou wouldst be at, old gentleman?   20

SIR TUNBELLY

I would be at you, sirrah (if my hands were not tied as a
magistrate), and with these two double fists beat your teeth
down your throat, you dog you!

LORD FOPPINGTON

And why wouldst thou spoil my face at that rate?

SIR TUNBELLY

For your design to rob me of my daughter, villain.   25

LORD FOPPINGTON

Rab thee of thy daughter! [*Aside*] Now do I begin to
believe I am a-bed and asleep, and that all this is but a
dream.—If it be, 'twill be an agreeable surprise enough to
waken by and by; and instead of the impertinent company of
a nasty country justice, find myself perhaps in the arms of   30
a woman of quality. (*To* SIR TUNBELLY) Prithee, old father,
wilt thou give me leave to ask thee one question?

SIR TUNBELLY

I can't tell whether I will or not, till I know what it is.

LORD FOPPINGTON

Why, then it is, whether thou didst not write to my Lord
Foppington to come down and marry thy daughter?   '   35

SIR TUNBELLY

Yes, marry did I; and my Lord Foppington is come down,
and shall marry my daughter before she's a day older.

LORD FOPPINGTON

Now give me thy hand, dear dad; I thought we should
understand one another at last.

SIR TUNBELLY

This fellow's mad.—Here, bind him hand and foot.   40
                              (*They bind him down*)

LORD FOPPINGTON

Nay, prithee, knight, leave fooling; thy jest begins to grow
dull.

SIR TUNBELLY

Bind him, I say, he's mad.—Bread and water, a dark room,
and a whip may bring him to his senses again.

LORD FOPPINGTON (*Aside*)

Egad! if I don't waken quickly, by all I can see, this is like   45 to prove one of the most impertinent dreams that ever I dreamt in my life.

Enter MISS HOYDEN *and* NURSE

HOYDEN (*Going up to him*)
Is this he that would have run away with me? Fo! how he stinks of sweets! Pray, father, let him be dragged through the horse-pond.   50
LORD FOPPINGTON (*Aside*)
This must be my wife by her natural inclination to her husband.
HOYDEN
Pray, father, what do you intend to do with him, hang him?
SIR TUNBELLY
That at least, child.
NURSE
Ay, and it's e'en too good for him, too.   55
LORD FOPPINGTON (*Aside*)
Madame la gouvernante, I presume. Hitherto this appears to me to be one of the most extraordinary families that ever man of quality matched into.
SIR TUNBELLY
What's become of my lord, daughter?
HOYDEN
He's just coming, sir.   60
LORD FOPPINGTON (*Aside*)
My lord? What does he mean by that now?

Enter YOUNG FASHION *and* LORY

(*Seeing him*)
Stap my vitals, Tam! Now the dream's out.
FASHION
Is this the fellow, sir, that designed to trick me of your daughter?
SIR TUNBELLY
This is he, my lord; how do you like him? Is not he a pretty   65
fellow to get a fortune?
FASHION
I find by his dress he thought your daughter might be taken with a beau.
HOYDEN
O Gemini! Is this a beau? Let me see him again.—Ha! I find a beau's no such an ugly thing neither.   70

FASHION [*Aside*]

Egad, she'll be in love with him presently; I'll e'en have him
sent away to jail.—(*To* LORD FOPPINGTON) Sir, though your
undertaking shows you are a person of no extraordinary
modesty, I suppose you han't confidence enough to expect
much favour from me?   75

LORD FOPPINGTON

Strike me dumb, Tam, thou art a very impudent fellow!

NURSE

Look, if the varlet has not the 'frontery to call his lordship
plain Thomas!

BULL

The business is, he would feign himself mad, to avoid going
to jail.   80

LORD FOPPINGTON (*Aside*)

That must be the chaplain, by his unfolding of mysteries.

SIR TUNBELLY

Come, is the warrant writ?

CLERK

Yes, sir.

SIR TUNBELLY

Give me the pen, I'll sign it.—So now, constable, away with
him.   85

LORD FOPPINGTON

Hold one moment, pray, gentlemen. My Lord Foppington,
shall I beg one word with your lordship?

NURSE

O ho, it's my lord with him now! See how afflictions will
humble folks.

HOYDEN

Pray, my lord, don't let him whisper too close, lest he bite   90
your ear off.

LORD FOPPINGTON

I am not altogether so hungry as your ladyship is pleased to
imagine. ([*Aside*] *to* YOUNG FASHION) Look you, Tam, I am
sensible I have not been so kind to you as I ought, but I
hope you'll forget what's passed, and accept of the five   95
thousand pounds I offer; thou mayst live in extreme splendour
with it, stap my vitals!

FASHION

It's a much easier matter to prevent a disease than to cure it;
a quarter of that sum would have secured your mistress;
twice as much won't redeem her.   (*Leaving him*)   100

SIR TUNBELLY

Well, what says he?

FASHION

Only the rascal offered me a bribe to let him go.

SIR TUNBELLY

Ay, he shall go, with a pox to him!—Lead on, constable.

LORD FOPPINGTON

One word more, and I have done.

SIR TUNBELLY

Before Gad! thou art an impudent fellow, to trouble the   105
court at this rate after thou art condemned; but speak once
for all.

LORD FOPPINGTON

Why then, once for all; I have at last luckily called to mind
that there is a gentleman of this country, who I believe cannot
live far from this place, if he were here would satisfy you,   110
I am Navelty, Baron of Foppington, with five thousand
pounds a year, and that fellow there, a rascal not worth a
groat.

SIR TUNBELLY

Very well; now, who is this honest gentleman you are so
well acquainted with? (*To* YOUNG FASHION) Come, sir, we   115
shall hamper him.

LORD FOPPINGTON

'Tis Sir John Friendly.

SIR TUNBELLY

So; he lives within half a mile, and came down into the
country but last night; this bold-faced fellow thought he had
been at London still, and so quoted him; now we shall dis-   120
play him in his colours: I'll send for Sir John immediately.
—Here, fellow, away presently, and desire my neighbour
he'll do me the favour to step over, upon an extraordinary
occasion.—And in the meanwhile you had best secure this
sharper in the gate-house.   [*Exit* SERVANT]   125

CONSTABLE

An't please your worship, he may chance to give us the
slip thence. If I were worthy to advise, I think the dog-
kennel's a surer place.

SIR TUNBELLY

With all my heart; anywhere.

LORD FOPPINGTON

Nay, for heaven's sake, sir! Do me the favour to put me in a   130
clean room, that I mayn't daub my clothes.

SIR TUNBELLY
Oh, when you have married my daughter, her estate will
afford you new ones. Away with him!
LORD FOPPINGTON
A dirty country justice is a barbarous magistrate, stap my
vitals.   (*Exit* CONSTABLE *with* LORD FOPPINGTON)   135
FASHION (*Aside*)
Egad, I must prevent this knight's coming, or the house
will grow soon too hot to hold me.—(*To* SIR TUNBELLY) Sir,
I fancy 'tis not worth while to trouble Sir John upon this
impertinent fellow's desire: I'll send and call the messenger
back.   140
SIR TUNBELLY
Nay, with all my heart; for, to be sure, he thought he was
far enough off, or the rogue would never have named him.

Enter SERVANT

SERVANT
Sir, I met Sir John just lighting at the gate; he's come to
wait upon you.
SIR TUNBELLY
Nay, then it happens as one could wish.   145
FASHION (*Aside*)
The devil it does!—Lory, you see how things are, here will
be a discovery presently, and we shall have our brains beat
out; for my brother will be sure to swear he don't know me:
therefore, run into the stable, take the two first horses you
can light on, I'll slip out at the back door, and we'll away   150
immediately.
LORY
What, and leave your lady, sir?
FASHION
There's no danger in that as long as I have taken possession;
I shall know how to treat with 'em well enough, if once I am
out of their reach. Away! I'll steal after thee.   155
                (*Exit* LORY; *his master follows him out at one
                door, as* SIR JOHN [FRIENDLY] *enters at t'other*)

Enter SIR JOHN

SIR TUNBELLY
Sir John, you are the welcomest man alive; I had just sent a
messenger to desire you'd step over, upon a very extra-
ordinary occasion. We are all in arms here.
SIR JOHN
How so?

SIR TUNBELLY

Why, you must know, a finical sort of a tawdry fellow here   160
(I don't know who the devil he is, not I) hearing, I suppose,
that the match was concluded between my Lord Foppington
and my girl Hoyden, comes impudently to the gate, with a
whole pack of rogues in liveries, and would have passed
upon me for his lordship; but what does I? I comes up to   165
him boldly at the head of his guards, takes him by the throat,
strikes up his heels, binds him hand and foot, dispatches a
warrant, and commits him prisoner to the dog-kennel.

SIR JOHN

So; but how do you know but this was my lord? For I was
told he set out from London the day before me, with a very   170
fine retinue, and intended to come directly hither.

SIR TUNBELLY

Why, now to show you how many lies people raise in that
damned town, he came two nights ago post, with only one
servant, and is now in the house with me. But you don't
know the cream of the jest yet; this same rogue (that   175
lies yonder neck and heels among the hounds), thinking you
were out of the country, quotes you for his acquaintance,
and said if you were here, you'd justify him to be Lord
Foppington, and I know not what.

SIR JOHN

Pray will you let me see him?   180

SIR TUNBELLY

Ay, that you shall presently.—Here, fetch the prisoner.

(*Exit* SERVANT)

SIR JOHN

I wish there ben't some mistake in this business.—Where's
my lord? I know him very well.

SIR TUNBELLY

He was here just now.—[*To* BULL] See for him, doctor; tell
him Sir John is here to wait upon him.   (*Exit* BULL)   185

SIR JOHN

I hope, Sir Tunbelly, the young lady is not married yet.

SIR TUNBELLY

No, things won't be ready this week. But why do you say
you hope she is not married?

SIR JOHN

Some foolish fancies only, perhaps I'm mistaken.

Re-enter BULL

184 s.d. BULL Chaplain (Q1) and hereafter.

BULL

Sir, his lordship is just rid out to take the air.   190

SIR TUNBELLY

To take the air! Is that his London breeding, to go take the
air when gentlemen come to visit him?

SIR JOHN

'Tis possible he might want it, he might not be well, some
sudden qualm perhaps.

[*Re*]-*enter* CONSTABLE, *&c., with* LORD FOPPINGTON

LORD FOPPINGTON

Stap my vitals, I'll have satisfaction!   195

SIR JOHN (*Running to him*)

My dear Lord Foppington!

LORD FOPPINGTON

Dear Friendly, thou art come in the critical minute, strike
me dumb!

SIR JOHN

Why, I little thought I should have found you in fetters.

LORD FOPPINGTON

Why, truly the world must do me the justice to confess, I   200
do use to appear a little more *dégagé*; but this old gentleman,
not liking the freedom of my air, has been pleased to skewer
down my arms like a rabbit.

SIR TUNBELLY

Is it then possible that this should be the true Lord
Foppington at last?   205

LORD FOPPINGTON

Why, what do you see in his face to make you doubt of it?
Sir, without presuming to have any extraordinary opinion
of my figure, give me leave to tell you, if you had seen as
many lords as I have done, you would not think it impossible a person of a worse *taille* than mine might be a   210
modern man of quality.

SIR TUNBELLY

Unbind him, slaves!—My lord, I'm struck dumb, I can
only beg pardon by signs; but if a sacrifice will appease you,
you shall have it.—Here, pursue this Tartar, bring him back.
—Away, I say!—A dog! Oons, I'll cut off his ears and his   215
tail, I'll draw out all his teeth, pull his skin over his head—
and—and what shall I do more?

201 *dégagé* nonchalant

SIR JOHN
He does indeed deserve to be made an example of.
LORD FOPPINGTON
He does deserve to be *châtré*, stap my vitals!
SIR TUNBELLY
May I then hope to have your honour's pardon?   220
LORD FOPPINGTON
Sir, we courtiers do nothing without a bribe: that fair young
lady might do miracles.
SIR TUNBELLY
Hoyden! come hither, Hoyden.
LORD FOPPINGTON
Hoyden is her name, sir?
SIR TUNBELLY
Yes, my lord.   225
LORD FOPPINGTON
The prettiest name for a song I ever heard.
SIR TUNBELLY
My lord—here's my girl; she's yours, she has a wholesome
body, and a virtuous mind; she's a woman complete, both
in flesh and in spirit; she has a bag of milled crowns, as
scarce as they are, and fifteen hundred a year stitched fast to   230
her tail: so, go thy ways, Hoyden.
LORD FOPPINGTON
Sir, I do receive her like a gentleman.
SIR TUNBELLY
Then I'm a happy man, I bless heaven, and if your lord-
ship will give me leave, I will, like a good Christian at
Christmas, be very drunk by way of thanksgiving. Come,   235
my noble peer, I believe dinner's ready; if your honour
pleases to follow me, I'll lead you on to the attack of a
venison-pasty.   (*Exit*)
LORD FOPPINGTON
Sir, I wait upon you.—Will your ladyship do me the favour
of your little finger, madam?   240
HOYDEN
My lord, I'll follow you presently. I have a little business
with my nurse.

219 *châtré* castrated. A. E. H. Swain's emendation of *chartre* (Q1), fully
     justified by his further reference to V, i, 37.
229 *milled crowns* These were replacing unmilled coins at this time in an
     attempt to prevent clipping and trimming.
231 *tail* probably punning upon entail, though Vanbrugh never makes
     clear the terms of Hoyden's fortune

LORD FOPPINGTON

Your ladyship's' most humble servant.—Come, Sir John; the ladies have *des affaires*.　　(*Exit with* SIR JOHN FRIENDLY)

HOYDEN

So, nurse, we are finely brought to bed! What shall we do 245 now?

NURSE

Ah, dear miss, we are all undone! Mr Bull, you were used to help a woman to a remedy.　　　　　　　　　　　　　(*Crying*)

BULL

Alack-a-day! but it's past my skill now, I can do nothing.

NURSE

Who would have thought that ever your invention should 250 have been drained so dry?

HOYDEN

Well, I have often thought old folks fools, and now I'm sure they are so; I have found a way myself to secure us all.

NURSE

Dear lady, what's that?

HOYDEN

Why, if you two will be sure to hold your tongues, and not 255 say a word of what's past, I'll e'en marry this lord, too.

NURSE

What! two husbands, my dear?

HOYDEN

Why, you have had three, good nurse, you may hold your tongue.

NURSE

Ay, but not altogether, sweet child.　　　　　　　　　　　260

HOYDEN

Psha! if you had, you'd ne'er a thought much on't.

NURSE

Oh, but 'tis a sin, sweeting!

BULL

Nay, that's my business to speak to, nurse.—I do confess, to take two husbands for the satisfaction of the flesh, is to commit the sin of exorbitancy; but to do it for the peace of 265 the spirit, is no more than to be drunk by way of physic. Besides, to prevent a parent's wrath, is to avoid the sin of disobedience; for when the parent's angry, the child is froward. So that upon the whole matter, I do think, though Miss should marry again, she may be saved.　　　　　　　270

266 *physic* medicine

5

HOYDEN
Ecod, and I will marry again then! and so there's an end of
the story.   [*Exeunt*]

Act V, Scene i

London
Enter COUPLER, YOUNG FASHION, *and* LORY

COUPLER
Well, and so Sir John coming in—
FASHION
And so Sir John coming in, I thought it might be manners in
me to go out, which I did, and getting on horseback as fast
as I could, rid away as if the devil had been at the rear of me.
What has happened since, heaven knows.   5
COUPLER
Egad, sirrah, I know as well as heaven.
FASHION
What do you know?
COUPLER
That you are a cuckold.
FASHION
The devil I am! By who?
COUPLER
By your brother.   10
FASHION
My brother! which way?
COUPLER
The old way; he has lain with your wife.
FASHION
Hell and furies! what dost thou mean?
COUPLER
I mean plainly; I speak no parable.
FASHION
Plainly! thou dost not speak common sense, I cannot under-   15
stand one word thou sayst.
COUPLER
You will do soon, youngster. In short, you left your wife a
widow, and she married again.
FASHION
It's a lie.

272 Q1 adds 'End of the Fourth ACT'.

COUPLER

Ecod, if I were a young fellow, I'd break your head, sirrah.   20

FASHION

Dear dad, don't be angry, for I'm as mad as Tom of Bedlam.

COUPLER

When I had fitted you with a wife, you should have kept her.

FASHION

But is it possible the young strumpet could play me such a
trick?

COUPLER

A young strumpet, sir, can play twenty tricks.   25

FASHION

But prithee instruct me a little farther; whence comes thy
intelligence?

COUPLER

From your brother, in this letter; there, you may read it.

FASHION (*Reads*)

Dear Coupler,—(Pulling off his hat) I have only time to tell
thee in three lines, or thereabouts, that here has been the devil.   30
That rascal Tam, having stole the letter thou hadst formerly writ
for me to bring to Sir Tunbelly, formed a damnable design upon
my mistress, and was in a fair way of success when I arrived.
But after having suffered some indignities (in which I have all
daubed my embroidered coat), I put him to flight. I sent out a   35
party of horse after him, in hopes to have made him my prisoner,
which if I had done, I would have qualified him for the seraglio,
stap my vitals!

The danger I have thus narrowly 'scaped has made me
fortify myself against farther attempts, by entering immedi-   40
ately into an association with the young lady, by which we
engage to stand by one another as long as we both shall live.

In short, the papers are sealed, and the contract is signed,
so the business of the lawyer is achevé; *but I defer the divine*
part of the thing till I arrive at London, not being willing to   45
consummate in any other bed but my own.

Postscript.

'Tis possible I may be in tawn as soon as this letter, far I find
the lady is so violently in love with me, I have determined
to make her happy with all the dispatch that is practicable,   50
without disardering my coach-harses.

So, here's rare work, i'faith!

22 *When* (1735) Then (Q1)

LORY

Egad, Miss Hoyden has laid about her bravely!

COUPLER

I think my country-girl has played her part as well as if she
had been born and bred in St James's parish.   55

FASHION

That rogue the chaplain!

LORY

And then that jade the nurse, sir!

FASHION

And then that drunken sot Lory, sir! that could not keep
himself sober to be a witness to the marriage.

LORY

Sir—with respect—I know very few drunken sots that do   60
keep themselves sober.

FASHION

Hold your prating, sirrah, or I'll break your head!—Dear
Coupler, what's to be done?

COUPLER

Nothing's to be done till the bride and bridegroom come to
town.   65

FASHION

Bride and bridegroom! death and furies! I can't bear that
thou shouldst call 'em so.

COUPLER

Why, what shall I call 'em, dog and cat?

FASHION

Not for the world, that sounds more like man and wife than
t'other.   70

COUPLER

Well, if you'll hear of 'em in no language, we'll leave 'em for
the nurse and the chaplain.

FASHION

The devil and the witch!

COUPLER

When they come to town—

LORY

We shall have stormy weather.   75

COUPLER

Will you hold your tongues, gentlemen, or not?

LORY

Mum.

COUPLER

I say when they come, we must find what stuff they are

made of, whether the churchman be chiefly composed of the
flesh, or the spirit; I presume the former. For as chaplains   80
now go, 'tis probable he eats three pound of beef to the
reading of one chapter.—This gives him carnal desires, he
wants money, preferment, wine, a whore; therefore we must
invite him to supper, give him fat capons, sack and sugar,
a purse of gold, and a plump sister. Let this be done, and   85
I'll warrant thee, my boy, he speaks truth like an oracle.

FASHION

Thou art a profound statesman I allow it; but how shall we
gain the nurse?

COUPLER

Oh, never fear the nurse, if once you have got the priest;
for the devil always rides the hag. Well, there's nothing   90
more to be said of the matter at this time, that I know of; so
let us go and inquire if there's any news of our people yet,
perhaps they may be come. But let me tell you one thing by
the way, sirrah, I doubt you have been an idle fellow; if
thou hadst behaved thyself as thou shouldst have done, the   95
girl would never have left thee.   (*Exeunt*)

Act V, Scene ii

BERINTHIA'S *apartment*
Enter her MAID, *passing the stage, followed by* WORTHY

WORTHY

Hem, Mrs Abigail, is your mistress to be spoken with?

ABIGAIL

By you, sir, I believe she may.

WORTHY

Why 'tis by me I would have her spoken with.

ABIGAIL

I'll acquaint her, sir.   (*Exit*)

WORTHY (*Solus*)

One lift more I must persuade her to give me, and then I'm   5
mounted. Well, a young bawd and a handsome one for my
money; 'tis they do the execution; I'll never go to an old
one, but when I have occasion for a witch. Lewdness looks
heavenly to a woman, when an angel appears in its cause; but
when a hag is advocate, she thinks it comes from the devil.   10
An old woman has something so terrible in her looks, that
whilst she is persuading your mistress to forget she has a
soul, she stares hell and damnation full in her face.

Enter BERINTHIA

BERINTHIA

Well, sir, what news brings you?

WORTHY

No news, madam; there's a woman going to cuckold her   15
husband.

BERINTHIA

Amanda?

WORTHY

I hope so.

BERINTHIA

Speed her well!

WORTHY

Ay, but there must be more than a God-speed, or your   20
charity won't be worth a farthing.

BERINTHIA

Why, han't I done enough already?

WORTHY

Not quite.

BERINTHIA

What's the matter?

WORTHY

The lady has a scruple still, which you must remove.   25

BERINTHIA

What's that?

WORTHY

Her virtue—she says.

BERINTHIA

And do you believe her?

WORTHY

No, but I believe it's what she takes for her virtue; it's some
relics of lawful love. She is not yet fully satisfied her husband   30
has got another mistress; which unless I can convince her of,
I have opened the trenches in vain; for the breach must be
wider, before I dare storm the town.

BERINTHIA

And so I'm to be your engineer?

WORTHY

I'm sure you know best how to manage the battery.   35

BERINTHIA

What think you of springing a mine? I have a thought just
now come into my head, how to blow her up at once.

WORTHY

That would be a thought indeed.

BERINTHIA

Faith, I'll do't; and thus the execution of it shall be. We are
all invited to my Lord Foppington's tonight to supper; he's   40
come to town with his bride, and makes a ball, with an
entertainment of music. Now, you must know, my undoer
here, Loveless, says he must needs meet me about some
private business (I don't know what 'tis) before we go to
the company. To which end he has told his wife one lie,   45
and I have told her another. But to make her amends, I'll
go immediately, and tell her a solemn truth.

WORTHY

What's that?

BERINTHIA

Why, I'll tell her that to my certain knowledge her husband
has a rendezvous with his mistress this afternoon; and that   50
if she'll give me her word she'll be satisfied with the discovery, without making any violent inquiry after the woman,
I'll direct her to a place where she shall see 'em meet. Now,
friend, this I fancy may help you to a critical minute. For
home she must go again to dress. You (with your good   55
breeding) come to wait upon us to the ball, find her all
alone, her spirit inflamed against her husband for his
treason, and her flesh in a heat from some contemplations
upon the treachery, her blood on a fire, her conscience in
ice; a lover to draw, and the devil to drive.—Ah, poor   60
Amanda!

WORTHY (*Kneeling*)

Thou angel of light, let me fall down and adore thee!

BERINTHIA

Thou minister of darkness, get up again, for I hate to see the
devil at his devotions.

WORTHY

Well, my incomparable Berinthia, how shall I requite you?   65

BERINTHIA

Oh, ne'er trouble yourself about that: virtue is its own
reward. There's a pleasure in doing good, which sufficiently
pays itself. Adieu!

WORTHY

Farewell, thou best of women!   (*Exeunt several ways*)

Enter AMANDA *meeting* BERINTHIA

AMANDA

Who was that went from you?   70

BERINTHIA

A friend of yours.

AMANDA

What does he want?

BERINTHIA

Something you might spare him, and be ne'er the poorer.

AMANDA

I can spare him nothing but my friendship; my love's
already disposed of, though, I confess, to one ungrateful   75
to my bounty.

BERINTHIA

Why, there's the mystery! You have been so bountiful, you
have cloyed him. Fond wives do by their husbands, as
barren wives do by their lapdogs; cram 'em with sweetmeats
till they spoil their stomachs.   80

AMANDA

Alas! had you but seen how passionately fond he has been
since our last reconciliation, you would have thought it
were impossible he ever should have breathed an hour
without me.

BERINTHIA

Ay, but there you thought wrong again, Amanda; you   85
should consider that in matters of love men's eyes are always
bigger than their bellies. They have violent appetites, 'tis
true, but they have soon dined.

AMANDA

Well; there's nothing upon earth astonishes me more than
men's inconstancy.   90

BERINTHIA

Now there's nothing upon earth astonishes me less, when I
consider what they and we are composed of. For nature has
made them children, and us babies. Now, Amanda, how we
used our babies you may remember. We were mad to have
'em as soon as we saw 'em; kissed 'em to pieces as soon as   95
we got 'em; then pulled off their clothes, saw 'em naked,
and so threw 'em away.

AMANDA

But do you think all men are of this temper?

BERINTHIA

All but one.

74–5 *love's already* love already's (Q1)
93 *babies* dolls

AMANDA
Who is that?   100
BERINTHIA
Worthy.
AMANDA
Why, he's weary of his wife too, you see.
BERINTHIA
Ay, that's no proof.
AMANDA
What can be a greater?
BERINTHIA
Being weary of his mistress.   105
AMANDA
Don't you think 'twere possible he might give you that, too?
BERINTHIA
Perhaps he might, if he were my gallant; not if he were
yours.
AMANDA
Why do you think he should be more constant to me, than
he would to you? I'm sure I'm not so handsome.   110
BERINTHIA
Kissing goes by favour; he likes you best.
AMANDA
Suppose he does? That's no demonstration he would be
constant to me.
BERINTHIA
No, that I'll grant you: but there are other reasons to expect
it. For you must know after all, Amanda, the inconstancy we   115
commonly see in men of brains, does not so much proceed
from the uncertainty of their temper, as from the misfortunes of their love. A man sees perhaps a hundred women
he likes well enough for an intrigue, and away, but possibly,
through the whole course of his life, does not find above one   120
who is exactly what he could wish her; now her, 'tis a
thousand to one, he never gets. Either she is not to be had at
all (though that seldom happens, you'll say), or he wants
those opportunities that are necessary to gain her. Either
she likes somebody else much better than him, or uses him   125
like a dog, because he likes nobody so well as her. Still
something or other Fate claps in the way between them and
the woman they are capable of being fond of; and this makes
them wander about from mistress to mistress, like a pilgrim
from town to town, who every night must have a fresh   130
lodging, and's in haste to be gone in the morning.

AMANDA

'Tis possible there may be something in what you say; but
what do you infer from it as to the man we were talking of?

BERINTHIA

Why, I infer, that you being the woman in the world the
most to his humour, 'tis not likely he would quit you for one   135
that is less.

AMANDA

That is not to be depended upon, for you see Mr Loveless
does so.

BERINTHIA

What does Mr Loveless do?

AMANDA

Why, he runs after something for variety I'm sure he does   140
not like so well as he does me.

BERINTHIA

That's more than you know, madam.

AMANDA

No, I'm sure on't. I'm not very vain, Berinthia, and yet I'd
lay my life, if I could look into his heart, he thinks I deserve
to be preferred to a thousand of her.   145

BERINTHIA

Don't be too positive in that neither; a million to one but she
has the same opinion of you. What would you give to see her?

AMANDA

Hang her, dirty trull!—Though I really believe she's so ugly
she'd cure me of my jealousy.

BERINTHIA

All the men of sense about town say she's handsome.   150

AMANDA

They are as often out in those things as any people.

BERINTHIA

Then I'll give you farther proof—all the women about town
say she's a fool. Now I hope you're convinced?

AMANDA

Whate'er she be, I'm satisfied he does not like her well
enough to bestow anything more than a little outward   155
gallantry upon her.

BERINTHIA

Outward gallantry!—(*Aside*) I can't bear this.—(*To* AMANDA)
Don't you think she's a woman to be fobbed off so. Come,
I'm too much your friend to suffer you should be thus
grossly imposed upon by a man who does not deserve the   160
least part about you, unless he knew how to set a greater

value upon it. Therefore, in one word, to my certain
knowledge, he is to meet her now, within a quarter of an
hour, somewhere about that Babylon of wickedness, Whitehall. And if you'll give me your word that you'll be content   165
with seeing her masked in his hand, without pulling her
headclothes off, I'll step immediately to the person from
whom I have my intelligence, and send you word where-
abouts you may stand to see 'em meet. My friend and I'll
watch 'em from another place, and dodge 'em to their   170
private lodging. But don't you offer to follow 'em, lest you
do it awkwardly, and spoil all. I'll come home to you again
as soon as I have earthed 'em, and give you an account in
what corner of the house the scene of their lewdness lies.

AMANDA
If you can do this, Berinthia, he's a villain.   175

BERINTHIA
I can't help that; men will be so.

AMANDA
Well! I'll follow your directions, for I shall never rest till
I know the worst of this matter.

BERINTHIA
Pray, go immediately and get yourself ready then. Put on
some of your woman's clothes, a great scarf and a mask, and   180
you shall presently receive orders.—(*Calls within*) Here,
who's there? Get me a chair quickly.

SERVANT [*Within*]
There are chairs at the door, madam.

BERINTHIA
'Tis well; I'm coming.

AMANDA
But pray, Berinthia, before you go, tell me how I may   185
know this filthy thing, if she should be so forward (as I
suppose she will) to come to the rendezvous first; for methinks I would fain view her a little.

BERINTHIA
Why, she's about my height; and very well shaped.

AMANDA
I thought she had been a little crooked?   190

BERINTHIA
Oh no, she's as straight as I am. But we lose time; come
away.   (*Exeunt*)

163 *her now* (CE) her; now (Q1)
173 *earthed* (CE) earth (Q1)
    earthed run to earth

Act V, Scene iii

Enter YOUNG FASHION, *meeting* LORY

FASHION

Well, will the doctor come?

LORY

Sir, I sent a porter to him as you ordered me. He found him
with a pipe of tobacco and a great tankard of ale, which he
said he would dispatch while I could tell three, and be here.

FASHION

He does not suspect 'twas I that sent for him?   5

LORY

Not a jot, sir; he divines as little for himself as he does for
other folks.

FASHION

Will he bring nurse with him?

LORY

Yes.

FASHION

That's well; where's Coupler?   10

LORY

He's half-way up the stairs taking breath; he must play his
bellows a little, before he can get to the top.

Enter COUPLER

FASHION

Oh, here he is.—Well, Old Phthisic, the doctor's coming.

COUPLER

Would the pox had the doctor!—I'm quite out of wind.—(*To*
LORY) Set me a chair, sirrah. Ah!—(*Sits down. To* YOUNG   15
FASHION) Why the plague canst not thou lodge upon the
ground floor?

FASHION

Because I love to lie as near heaven as I can.

COUPLER

Prithee let heaven alone; ne'er affect tending that way; thy
centre's downwards.   20

FASHION

That's impossible. I have too much ill-luck in this world to
be damned in the next.

---

1 *come?* This scene is presumably in Young Fashion's lodgings.
13 *Phthisic* asthmatic

COUPLER

    Thou art out in thy logic. Thy major is true, but thy minor is
false; for thou art the luckiest fellow in the universe.

FASHION

    Make out that.   25

COUPLER

    I'll do't: last night the devil ran away with the parson of
Fatgoose living.

FASHION

    If he had run away with the parish too, what's that to me?

COUPLER

    I'll tell thee what it's to thee.—This living is worth five
hundred pound a year, and the presentation of it is thine, if   30
thou canst prove thyself a lawful husband to Miss Hoyden.

FASHION

    Say'st thou so, my protector? Then, egad, I shall have a
brace of evidences here presently.

COUPLER

    The nurse and the doctor?

FASHION

    The same. The devil himself won't have interest enough to   35
make 'em withstand it.

COUPLER

    That we shall see presently.—Here they come.

Enter NURSE *and* CHAPLAIN; *they start back
seeing* YOUNG FASHION

NURSE

    Ah, goodness, Roger, we are betrayed!

FASHION (*Laying hold on 'em*)

    Nay, nay, ne'er flinch for the matter, for I have you safe.
Come, to your trials immediately; I have no time to give   40
you copies of your indictment. There sits your judge.

BOTH (*Kneeling*)

    Pray, sir, have compassion on us.

NURSE

    I hope, sir, my years will move your pity; I am an aged woman.

COUPLER

    That is a moving argument indeed.

BULL

    I hope, sir, my character will be considered; I am heaven's   45
ambassador.

COUPLER [*To* BULL]

    Are not you a rogue of sanctity?

BULL

Sir (with respect to my function), I do wear a gown.

COUPLER

Did not you marry this vigorous young fellow to a plump
young buxom wench?   50

NURSE (*Aside to* BULL)

Don't confess, Roger, unless you are hard put to it indeed.

COUPLER

Come, out with't!—Now is he chewing the cud of his
roguery, and grinding a lie between his teeth.

BULL

Sir,—I cannot positively say—I say, sir,—positively I
cannot say.   55

COUPLER

Come, no equivocations, no Roman turns upon us. Consider thou standest upon Protestant ground, which will slip
from under thee like a Tyburn cart; for in this country we
have always ten hangmen for one Jesuit.

BULL (*To* YOUNG FASHION)

Pray, sir, then will you but permit me to speak one word in   60
private with nurse?

FASHION

Thou art always for doing something in private with nurse.

COUPLER

But pray let his betters be served before him for once. I
would do something in private with her myself. Lory,
take care of this reverend gownman in the next room a little.   65
—Retire, priest. (*Exit* LORY *with* BULL) Now, virgin, I must
put the matter home to you a little. Do you think it might
not be possible to make you speak truth?

NURSE

Alas, sir! I don't know what you mean by truth.

COUPLER

Nay, 'tis possible thou mayst be a stranger to it.   70

FASHION

Come, nurse, you and I were better friends when we saw one
another last; and I still believe you are a very good woman in
the bottom. I did deceive you and your young lady, 'tis true,
but I always designed to make a very good husband to her,
and to be a very good friend to you. And 'tis possible, in the   75

---

56 *equivocations* saying one thing while meaning another, a practice
   alleged to have been common among Roman Catholics, and to
   have been condoned by the Jesuits, in penal times

end, she might have found herself happier, and you richer,
than ever my brother will make you.

NURSE

Brother! why is your worship then his lordship's brother?

FASHION

I am; which you should have known, if I durst have stayed
to have told you; but I was forced to take horse a little in   80
haste, you know.

NURSE

You were indeed, sir: poor young man, how he was bound
to scour for't! Now won't your worship be angry, if I
confess the truth to you? When I found you were a cheat
(with respect be it spoken), I verily believed Miss had got   85
some pitiful skip-jack varlet or other to her husband, or I
had ne'er let her think of marrying again.

COUPLER

But where was your conscience all this while, woman? Did
not that stare in your face with huge saucer-eyes, and a great
horn upon the forehead? Did not you think you should be   90
damned for such a sin?—Ha?

FASHION

Well said, divinity! Press that home upon her.

NURSE

Why, in good truly, sir, I had some fearful thoughts on't, and
could never be brought to consent, till Mr Bull said it was
a *peckadilla*, and he'd secure my soul for a tithe-pig.   95

FASHION

There was a rogue for you!

COUPLER

And he shall thrive accordingly. He shall have a good living.
—Come, honest nurse, I see you have butter in your compound; you can melt. Some compassion you can have of this
handsome young fellow.   100

NURSE

I have, indeed, sir.

FASHION

Why then, I'll tell you what you shall do for me. You know
what a warm living here is fallen; and that it must be in
the disposal of him who has the disposal of Miss. Now if

83 *scour* run
86 *skip-jack* professional deceiver, fly-by-night
92 *Press* (1735) Pass (Q1)
95 *peckadilla* peccadillo

you and the doctor will agree to prove my marriage, I'll 105
present him to it, upon condition he makes you his bride.

NURSE

Naw the blessing of the Lord follow your good worship
both by night and by day! Let him be fetched in by the ears;
I'll soon bring his nose to the grindstone.

COUPLER (*Aside*)

Well said, old white-leather!—[*Aloud*] Hey, bring in the 110
prisoner there!

Enter LORY *with* BULL

COUPLER

Come, advance, holy man. Here's your duck does not think
fit to retire with you into the chancel at this time; but she
has a proposal to make to you in the face of the congregation.
Come, nurse, speak for yourself, you are of age. 115

NURSE

Roger, are not you a wicked man, Roger, to set your strength
against a weak woman, and persuade her it was no sin to
conceal Miss's nuptials? My conscience flies in my face for
it, thou priest of Baal! and I find by woeful experience, thy
absolution is not worth an old cassock. Therefore I am 120
resolved to confess the truth to the whole world, though I
die a beggar for it. But his worship overflows with his
mercy and his bounty; he is not only pleased to forgive us
our sins, but designs thou sha't squat thee down in Fatgoose living; and which is more than all, has prevailed with 125
me to become the wife of thy bosom.

FASHION

All this I intend for you, doctor. What you are to do for me,
I need not tell you.

BULL

Your worship's goodness is unspeakable. Yet there is one
thing seems a point of conscience; and conscience is a 130
tender babe. If I should bind myself, for the sake of this
living, to marry nurse, and maintain her afterwards, I
doubt it might be looked on as a kind of simony.

COUPLER (*Rising up*)

If it were sacrilege, the living's worth it: therefore no more

110 *white-leather* leather specially prepared by scourging, with alum
    and salt as ingredients of treatment; Coupler probably uses the
    expression to convey the hypocrisy of Nurse's transformation.
119 *Baal* Bale (Q1) false god (Bale obsolete form of Baal)

words, good doctor; but with the parish—(*Giving* NURSE *to*   135
him) here—take the parsonage-house. 'Tis true, 'tis a little
out of repair; some dilapidations there are to be made good;
the windows are broke, the wainscot is warped, the ceilings
are peeled, and the walls are cracked; but a little glazing,
painting, whitewash, and plaster, will make it last thy time.   140

BULL
Well, sir, if it must be so, I shan't contend. What Providence
orders, I submit to.

NURSE
And so do I, with all humility.

COUPLER
Why, that now was spoke like good people. Come, my
turtle-doves, let us go help this poor pigeon to his wander-   145
ing mate again; and after institution and induction, you shall
all go a-cooing together.   (*Exeunt*)

Act V, Scene iv

Enter AMANDA *in a scarf, &c., as just returned,
her* WOMAN *following her*

AMANDA
Prithee, what care I who has been here?

WOMAN
Madam, 'twas my Lady Bridle and my Lady Tiptoe.

AMANDA
My Lady Fiddle and my Lady Faddle! What does stand
troubling me with the visits of a parcel of impertinent
women? When they are well seamed with the small-pox, they   5
won't be so fond of showing their faces. There are more
coquettes about this town—

WOMAN
Madam, I suppose they only came to return your ladyship's
visit, according to the custom of the world.

AMANDA
Would the world were on fire, and you in the middle on't!   10
Begone. Leave me.—(*Exit* WOMAN)
                        Sola
At last I am convinced. My eyes are testimonies of his
falsehood. The base, ungrateful, perjured villain!—
Good gods! what slippery stuff are men compos'd of!
Sure the account of their creation's false,   15

s.d. *as just returned* presumably to Loveless's lodgings

And 'twas the woman's rib that they were form'd of.
But why am I thus angry?
This poor relapse should only move my scorn.
'Tis true, the roving flights of his unfinished youth
Had strong excuse from the plea of nature;   20
Reason had thrown the reins loose on his neck,
And slipped him to unlimited desire.
If therefore he went wrong, he had a claim
To my forgiveness, and I did him right.
But since the years of manhood rein him in,   25
And reason, well digested into thought,
Has pointed out the course he ought to run;
If now he strays,
'Twould be as weak and mean in me to pardon,
As it had been in him t'offend. But hold: 30
'Tis an ill cause indeed, where nothing's to be said for't.
My beauty possibly is in the wane;
Perhaps sixteen has greater charms for him:
Yes, there's the secret. But let him know,
My quiver's not entirely emptied yet,   35
I still have darts, and I can shoot 'em too;
They're not so blunt, but they can enter still:
The want's not in my power, but in my will.
Virtue's his friend; or, through another's heart,
I yet could find the way to make his smart.   40

(*Going off, she meets* WORTHY)

Ha! he here?
Protect me, heaven, for this looks ominous.

[*Enter* WORTHY]

WORTHY
You seem disordered, madam;
I hope there's no misfortune happened to you?
AMANDA
None that will long disorder me, I hope.
WORTHY
Whate'er it be disturbs you, I would to heaven
'Twere in my power to bear the pain,
Till I were able to remove the cause.
AMANDA
I hope ere long it will remove itself.
At least, I have given it warning to be gone.   50
WORTHY
Would I durst ask, where 'tis the thorn torments you?

Forgive me, if I grow inquisitive;
'Tis only with desire to give you ease.

AMANDA

Alas! 'tis in a tender part.
It can't be drawn without a world of pain.   55
Yet out it must;
For it begins to fester in my heart.

WORTHY

If 'tis the sting of unrequited love, remove it instantly:
I have a balm will quickly heal the wound.

AMANDA

You'll find the undertaking difficult.   60
The surgeon, who already has attempted it,
Has much tormented me.

WORTHY

I'll aid him with a gentler hand,
—If you will give me leave.

AMANDA

How soft soe'er the hand may be,   65
There still is terror in the operation.

WORTHY

Some few preparatives would make it easy, could I persuade
you to apply 'em. Make home reflections, madam, on your
slighted love. Weigh well the strength and beauty of your
charms: rouse up that spirit women ought to bear, and   70
slight your god, if he neglects his angel. With arms of ice
receive his cold embraces, and keep your fire for those who
come in flames. Behold a burning lover at your feet, his fever
raging in his veins! See how he trembles, how he pants! See
how he glows, how he consumes! Extend the arms of mercy   75
to his aid; his zeal may give him title to your pity, although
his merit cannot claim your love.

AMANDA

Of all my feeble sex, sure I must be the weakest, should I
again presume to think on love. (*Sighing*) Alas! my heart
has been too roughly treated.   80

WORTHY

'Twill find the greater bliss in softer usage.

AMANDA

But where's that usage to be found?

WORTHY

'Tis here, within this faithful breast; which if you doubt,

68 *home reflections* reflections that evoke home truths

I'll rip it up before your eyes; lay all its secrets open to your
view; and then, you'll see 'twas sound.   85

AMANDA

With just such honest words as these, the worst of men
deceived me.

WORTHY

He therefore merits all revenge can do; his fault is such, the
extent and stretch of vengeance cannot reach it. Oh, make
me but your instrument of justice; you'll find me execute it   90
with such zeal, as shall convince you I abhor the crime.

AMANDA

The rigour of an executioner has more the face of cruelty
than justice: and he who puts the cord about the wretch's
neck, is seldom known to exceed him in his morals.

WORTHY

What proof then can I give you of my truth?   95

AMANDA

There is on earth but one.

WORTHY

And is that in my power?

AMANDA

It is: and one that would so thoroughly convince me, I
should be apt to rate your heart so high, I possibly might
purchase't with a part of mine.   100

WORTHY

Then heaven, thou art my friend, and I am blest; for if 'tis
in my power, my will I'm sure will reach it. No matter what
the terms may be, when such a recompense is offer'd. Oh, tell
me quickly what this proof must be. What is it will convince
you of my love?   105

AMANDA

I shall believe you love me as you ought, if, from this
moment you forbear to ask whatever is unfit for me to
grant.—You pause upon it, sir.—I doubt, on such hard
terms, a woman's heart is scarcely worth the having.

WORTHY

A heart, like yours, on any terms is worth it; 'twas not on   110
that I paused. But I was thinking (*Drawing nearer to her*)
whether some things there may not be, which women cannot grant without a blush, and yet which men may take
without offence. (*Taking her hand*) Your hand, I fancy, may
be of the number. Oh, pardon me, if I commit a rape   115
upon't (*Kissing it eagerly*); and thus devour it with my
kisses.

AMANDA

O Heavens! let me go.

WORTHY

Never, whilst I have strength to hold you here. (*Forcing her to sit down on a couch*) My life, my soul, my goddess—Oh, 120 forgive me!

AMANDA

Oh whither am I going? Help, Heaven, or I am lost.

WORTHY

Stand neuter, gods, this once, I do invoke you.

AMANDA

Then save me, virtue, and the glory's thine.

WORTHY

Nay, never strive.   125

AMANDA

I will, and conquer too. My forces rally bravely to my aid, (*Breaking from him*) and thus I gain the day.

WORTHY

Then mine as bravely double their attack; (*Seizing her again*) and thus I wrest it from you. Nay struggle not; for all's in vain: or death or victory, I am determined.   130

AMANDA

And so am I. (*Rushing from him*) Now keep your distance, or we part forever.

WORTHY (*Offering again*)

For heaven's sake!—

AMANDA (*Going*)

Nay then, farewell!

WORTHY

(*Kneeling, and holding by her clothes*) Oh stay! and see the 135 magic force of love. Behold this raging lion at your feet, struck dead with fear, and tame as charms can make him. What must I do to be forgiven by you?

AMANDA

Repent, and never more offend.

WORTHY

Repentance for past crimes is just and easy; but sin no more's 140 a task too hard for mortals.

AMANDA

Yet those who hope for heaven must use their best endeavours to perform it.

WORTHY

Endeavours we may use, but flesh and blood are got in t'other scale; and they are ponderous things.   145

AMANDA

Whate'er they are, there is a weight in resolution sufficient
for their balance. The soul, I do confess, is usually so
careless of its charge, so soft, and so indulgent to desire, it
leaves the reins in the wild hand of nature, who like a
Phaeton, drives the fiery chariot, and sets the world on flame. 150
Yet still the sovereignty is in the mind, whene'er it pleases to
exert its force. Perhaps you may not think it worth your
while to take such mighty pains for my esteem; but that I
leave to you.
You see the price I set upon my heart; 155
Perhaps 'tis dear: but, spite of all your art
You'll find on cheaper terms we n'er shall part. (*Exit*)

WORTHY (*Solus*)

Sure there's divinity about her. And sh'as dispensed some
portion on't to me. For what but now was the wild flame
of love, or (to dissect that specious term) the vile, the gross 160
desires of flesh and blood, is in a moment turned to adora-
tion. The coarser appetite of nature's gone, and 'tis,
methinks, the food of angels I require. How long this
influence may last, heaven knows, but in this moment of
my purity, I could on her own terms accept her heart. Yes, 165
lovely woman! I can accept it. For now 'tis doubly worth
my care. Your charms are much increased, since thus
adorned. When truth's extorted from us, then we own the
robe of virtue is a graceful habit.
Could women but our secret counsels scan, 170
Could they but reach the deep reserves of man,
They'd wear it on, that that of love might last;
For when they throw off one, we soon the other cast.
Their sympathy is such—
The fate of one, the other scarce can fly; 175
They live together, and together die. (*Exit*)

Act V, Scene v

Enter MISS HOYDEN *and* NURSE

HOYDEN

But is it sure and certain, say you, he's my lord's own
brother?

150 *Phaeton ... flame* Dobrée sees in this passage a reminiscence of
the *Phaedrus*.
157 *part* part with
s.d. This final scene takes place in Lord Foppington's house.

NURSE

As sure as he's your lawful husband.

HOYDEN

Ecod, if I had known that in time, I don't know but I might
have kept him: for, between you and I, nurse, he'd have   5
made a husband worth two of this I have. But which do you
think you should fancy most, nurse?

NURSE

Why, truly, in my poor fancy, madam, your first husband is
the prettier gentleman.

HOYDEN

I don't like my lord's shapes, nurse.   10

NURSE

Why, in good truly, as a body may say, he is but a slam.

HOYDEN

What do you think now he puts me in mind of? Don't you
remember a long, loose, shambling sort of a horse my father
called Washy?

NURSE

As like as two twin-brothers!   15

HOYDEN

Ecod, I have thought so a hundred times: faith, I'm tired of
him.

NURSE

Indeed, madam, I think you had e'en as good stand to your
first bargain.

HOYDEN

Oh, but nurse, we han't considered the main thing yet. If I   20
leave my lord, I must leave my lady, too; and when I rattle
about the streets in my coach, they'll only say, There goes
mistress—mistress—mistress what? What's this man's name
I have married, nurse?

NURSE

Squire Fashion.   25

HOYDEN

Squire Fashion is it? Well, Squire, that's better than nothing.
Do you think one could not get him made a knight, nurse?

NURSE

I don't know but one might, madam, when the king's in a
good humour.

HOYDEN

Ecod, that would do rarely. For then he'd be as good a man   30
as my father, you know.

11 *slam* an ungainly person (largely on this quotation)

NURSE

By'r Lady, and that's as good as the best of 'em.

HOYDEN

So 'tis, faith; for then I shall be my lady, and your ladyship, at every word, and that's all I have to care for. Ha,
nurse, but hark you me; one thing more and then I have   35
done. I'm afraid, if I change my husband again, I shan't
have so much money to throw about, nurse.

NURSE

Oh, enough's as good as a feast. Besides, madam, one don't
know but as much may fall to your share with the younger
brother as with the elder. For though these lords have a   40
power of wealth indeed, yet, as I have heard say, they give
it all to their sluts and their trulls, who joggle it about in
their coaches, with a murrain to 'em! whilst poor madam
sits sighing, and wishing, and knotting, and crying, and
has not a spare half-crown to buy her a *Practice of Piety*. 45

HOYDEN

Oh, but for that don't deceive yourself, nurse. For this I
must say for my lord, and a (*Snapping her fingers*) for him;
he's as free as an open house at Christmas. For this very
morning he told me I should have two hundred a year to buy
pins. Now, nurse, if he gives me two hundred a year to buy   50
pins, what do you think he'll give me to buy fine petticoats?

NURSE

Ah, my dearest, he deceives thee faully, and he's no better
than a rogue for his pains! These Londoners have got a
gibberidge with 'em would confound a gypsy. That which
they call pin-money is to buy their wives everything in the   55
'varsal world, down to their very shoe-ties. Nay, I have
heard folks say, that some ladies, if they will have gallants, as
they call 'em, are forced to find them out of their pin-money
too.

HOYDEN

Has he served me so, say ye?—Then I'll be his wife no   60
longer, so that's fixed. Look, here he comes, with all the fine

43 *murrain* plague
45 *Practice of Piety* a popular religious manual by Lewis Bayley,
   often mockingly alluded to in the drama. (See Montague Sum-
   mers's *Congreve*, I, 253)
52 *faully* presumably an attempt at dialect speech
54 *gibberidge* gibberish
56 *'varsal* universal

folk at's heels. Ecod, nurse, these London ladies will laugh
till they crack again, to see me slip my collar, and run away
from my husband. But, d'ye hear? Pray, take care of one
thing: when the business comes to break out, be sure you   65
get between me and my father, for you know his tricks; he'll
knock me down.

NURSE
I'll mind him, ne'er fear, madam.

> *Enter* LORD FOPPINGTON, LOVELESS, WORTHY,
> AMANDA, *and* BERINTHIA

LORD FOPPINGTON
Ladies and gentlemen, you are all welcome.—Loveless,
that's my wife; prithee do me the favour to salute her; and   70
dost hear (*Aside to him*) if thau hast a mind to try thy fartune,
to be revenged of me, I won't take it ill, stap my vitals!

LOVELESS
You need not fear, sir; I'm too fond of my own wife to
have the least inclination to yours. (*All salute* MISS HOYDEN)

LORD FOPPINGTON (*Aside*)
I'd give you a thousand paund he would make love to her,   75
that he may see she has sense enough to prefer me to him,
though his own wife has not. (*Viewing him*) He's a very
beastly fellow, in my opinion.

HOYDEN (*Aside*)
What a power of fine men there are in this London! He that
kissed me first is a goodly gentleman, I promise you. Sure   80
those wives have a rare time on't that live here always.

> *Enter* SIR TUNBELLY CLUMSEY, *with* MUSICIANS,
> DANCERS, &c.

SIR TUNBELLY
Come, come in, good people, come in! Come, tune your
fiddles, tune your fiddles!—(*To the* HAUTBOYS) Bagpipes,
make ready there. Come, strike up. (*Sings*)
> For this is HOYDEN's *wedding-day,*   85
> *And therefore we keep holiday,*
> *And come to be merry.*

Ha! there's my wench, i'faith. Touch and take, I'll warrant
her; she'll breed like a tame rabbit.

HOYDEN (*Aside*)
Ecod, I think my father's gotten drunk before supper.   90

86 *holiday* Holy-day (Q1)

SIR TUNBELLY

(*To* LOVELESS *and* WORTHY) Gentlemen, you are welcome.—
(*Saluting* AMANDA *and* BERINTHIA) Ladies, by your leave.—
(*Aside*) Ha! they bill like turtles. Udsookers, they set my old
blood a-fire; I shall cuckold somebody before morning.

LORD FOPPINGTON (*To* SIR TUNBELLY)

Sir, you being master of the entertainment, will you desire   95
the company to sit?

SIR TUNBELLY

Oons, sir, I'm the happiest man on this side the Ganges!

LORD FOPPINGTON (*Aside*)

This is a mighty unaccountable old fellow. (*To* SIR TUNBELLY)
I said, sir, it would be convenient to ask the company to sit.

SIR TUNBELLY

Sit?—with all my heart.—Come, take your places, ladies;   100
take your places, gentlemen.—Come, sit down, sit down;
a pox of ceremony! take your places.

(*They sit and the masque begins*)

DIALOGUE BETWEEN CUPID AND HYMEN
1

CUPID

Thou bane to my empire, thou spring of contest,
Thou source of all discord, thou period to rest,
Instruct me, what wretches in bondage can see,   105
That the aim of their life is still pointed to thee.

2

HYMEN

Instruct me, thou little, impertinent god,
From whence all thy subjects have taken the mode
To grow fond of a change, to whatever it be,
And I'll tell thee why those would be bound who are free.   110

CHORUS

For change, we're for change, to whatever it be,
We are neither contented with freedom nor thee.
　　　Constancy's an empty sound,
　　　Heaven, and earth, and all go round,
　　　All the works of Nature move,   115
　　　And the joys of life and love
　　　　　Are in variety.

3

CUPID

Were love the reward of a painstaking life,
Had a husband the art to be fond of his wife,

Were virtue so plenty, a wife could afford,   120
These very hard times, to be true to her lord,
Some specious account might be given of those
Who are tied by the tail, to be led by the nose.
                              4
But since 'tis the fate of a man and his wife,
To consume all their days in contention and strife;   125
Since, whatever the bounty of heaven may create her,
He's morally sure he shall heartily hate her,
I think 'twere much wiser to ramble at large,
And the volleys of love on the herd to discharge.
                              5

HYMEN
Some colour of reason thy counsel might bear,   130
Could a man have no more than his wife to his share:
Or were I a monarch so cruelly just,
To oblige a poor wife to be true to her trust;
But I have not pretended, for many years past,
By marrying of people, to make 'em grow chaste.   135
                              6
I therefore advise thee to let me go on,
Thou'lt find I'm the strength and support of thy throne:
For hadst thou but eyes, thou wouldst quickly perceive it,
        How smoothly the dart
        Slips into the heart   140
        Of a woman's that's wed;
        Whilst the shivering maid
Stands trembling, and wishing, but dare not receive it.

                          CHORUS
For change &.

(*The masque ended, enter* YOUNG FASHION, COUPLER, *and* BULL)

SIR TUNBELLY
So; very fine, very fine, i'faith! this is something like a   145
wedding. Now, if supper were but ready, I'd say a short
grace; and if I had such a bedfellow as Hoyden tonight—I'd
say as short prayers. (*Seeing* YOUNG FASHION) How now?—
What have we got here? A ghost? Nay, it must be so, for
his flesh and his blood could never have dared to appear   150
before me.—(*To him*) Ah, rogue!
LORD FOPPINGTON
Stap my vitals, Tam again.
SIR TUNBELLY
My lord, will you cut his throat, or shall I?

LORD FOPPINGTON

Leave him to me, sir, if you please.—Prithee, Tam, be so
ingenuous now as to tell me what thy business is here? 155

FASHION

'Tis with your bride.

LORD FOPPINGTON

Thau art the impudentest fellow that Nature has yet spawned
into the warld, strike me speechless!

FASHION

Why, you know my modesty would have starved me; I sent
it a-begging to you, and you would not give it a groat. 160

LORD FOPPINGTON

And dost thau expect by an excess of assurance to extart a
maintenance fram me?

FASHION (*Taking* MISS HOYDEN *by the hand*)

I do intend to extort your mistress from you, and that I hope
will prove one.

LORD FOPPINGTON

I ever thaught Newgate or Bedlam would be his fartune, and 165
naw his fate's decided. Prithee, Loveless, dost know of ever
a mad doctor hard by?

FASHION

There's one at your elbow will cure you presently. (*To*
BULL) Prithee, doctor, take him in hand quickly.

LORD FOPPINGTON

Shall I beg the favour of you, sir, to pull your fingers out of 170
my wife's hand?

FASHION

His wife! Look you there; now I hope you are all satisfied
he's mad.

LORD FOPPINGTON

Naw is it nat possible far me to penetrate what species of
fally it is thau art driving at! 175

SIR TUNBELLY

Here, here, here, let me beat out his brains, and that will
decide all.

LORD FOPPINGTON

No; pray, sir, hold, we'll destray him presently accarding to
law.

FASHION (*To* BULL)

Nay, then advance, doctor. Come, you are a man of con- 180
science, answer boldly to the questions I shall ask. Did you
not marry me to this young lady before ever that gentleman
there saw her face?

BULL
  Since the truth must out—I did.
FASHION
  Nurse, sweet nurse, were not you a witness to it?   185
NURSE
  Since my conscience bids me speak—I was.
FASHION (*To* MISS HOYDEN)
  Madam, am not I your lawful husband?
HOYDEN
  Truly I can't tell, but you married me first.
FASHION
  Now I hope you are all satisfied?
SIR TUNBELLY (*Offering to strike him, is held by* LOVELESS *and*
  WORTHY)
  Oons and thunder, you lie!   190
LORD FOPPINGTON
  Pray, sir, be calm; the battle is in disorder, but requires
  more canduct than courage to rally our forces.—Pray, dactar,
  one word with you.—(*To* BULL *aside*) Look you, sir, though
  I will not presume to calculate your notions of damnation
  fram the description you give us of hell, yet since there is at   195
  least a passibility you may have a pitch-fark thrust in your
  backside, methinks it should not be worth your while to
  risk your saul in the next warld, for the sake of a beggarly,
  yaunger brather, who is nat able to make your bady happy
  in this.   200
BULL
  Alas! my lord, I have no worldly ends; I speak the truth,
  heaven knows.
LORD FOPPINGTON
  Nay, prithee, never engage heaven in the matter, for by all I
  can see, 'tis like to prove a business for the devil.
FASHION
  Come, pray, sir, all above-board; no corrupting of evidences,   205
  if you please. This young lady is my lawful wife, and I'll
  justify it in all the courts of England; so your lordship (who
  always had a passion for variety) may go seek a new mistress
  if you think fit.
LORD FOPPINGTON
  I am struck dumb with his impudence, and cannot pasi-   210
  tively tell whether ever I shall speak again or nat.
SIR TUNBELLY
  Then let me come and examine the business a little, I'll jerk
  the truth out of 'em presently. Here, give me my dog-whip.

FASHION

Look you, old gentleman, 'tis in vain to make a noise; if you
grow mutinous, I have some friends within call, have swords   215
by their sides above four foot long; therefore be calm, hear
the evidence patiently, and when the jury have given their
verdict, pass sentence according to law. Here's honest
Coupler shall be foreman, and ask as many questions as he
pleases.   220

COUPLER

All I have to ask is, whether nurse persists in her evidence?
The parson, I dare swear, will never flinch from his.

NURSE (*To* SIR TUNBELLY, *kneeling*)

I hope in heaven your worship will pardon me. I have served
you long and faithfully, but in this thing I was over-reached;
your worship, however, was deceived as well as I, and if the   225
wedding-dinner had been ready, you had put madam to
bed to him with your own hands.

SIR TUNBELLY

But how durst you do this, without acquainting of me?

NURSE

Alas! If your worship had seen how the poor thing begged,
and prayed, and clung, and twined about me, like ivy to an   230
old wall, you would say, I who had suckled it, and swaddled
it, and nursed it both wet and dry, must have had a heart
of adamant to refuse it.

SIR TUNBELLY

Very well.

FASHION

Foreman, I expect your verdict.   235

COUPLER

Ladies and gentlemen, what's your opinions?

ALL

A clear case, a clear case.

COUPLER

Then, my young folks, I wish you joy.

SIR TUNBELLY (*To* YOUNG FASHION)

Come hither, stripling; if it be true then, that thou hast
married my daughter, prithee tell me who thou art?   240

FASHION

Sir, the best of my condition is, I am your son-in-law; and
the worst of it is, I am brother to that noble peer there.

SIR TUNBELLY

Art thou brother to that noble peer?—Why, then, that noble

peer, and thee, and thy wife, and the nurse, and the priest—
may all go and be damned together.   (*Exit*) 245
LORD FOPPINGTON (*Aside*)
Now for my part, I think the wisest thing a man can do with
an aching heart is to put on a serene countenance, for a
philosophical air is the most becoming thing in the world to
the face of a person of quality. I will therefore bear my
disgrace like a great man, and let the people see I am above 250
an affront. (*To* YOUNG FASHION) Dear Tam, since things
are thus fallen aut, prithee give me leave to wish thee jay;
I do it *de bon coeur*, strike me dumb! You have married a
woman beautiful in her person, charming in her airs, prudent
in her canduct, canstant in her inclinations, and of a nice 255
marality, split my windpipe!
FASHION
Your lordship may keep up your spirits with your grimace if
you please; I shall support mine with this lady, and two
thousand pound a year.—(*Taking* MISS HOYDEN'*s hand*)
Come, madam:—   260
We once again, you see, are man and wife,
And now, perhaps, the bargain's struck for life.
If I mistake, and we should part again,
At least you see you may have choice of men:
Nay, should the war at length such havoc make,   265
That lovers should grow scarce, yet for your sake,
Kind heaven always will preserve a beau:
(*Pointing to* LORD FOPPINGTON)
You'll find his lordship ready to come to.
LORD FOPPINGTON
Her ladyship shall stap my vitals, if I do.   (*Exeunt*)

259 s.d. (*Taking* MISS HOYDEN's *hand*) (*Taking* MISS) (Q1)

EPILOGUE

Spoken by LORD FOPPINGTON

Gentlemen and Ladies,
These people have regaled you here today
(In my opinion) with a saucy play;
In which the author does presume to show,
That coxcomb, *ab origine*—was beau.   5
Truly, I think the thing of so much weight,
That if some sharp chastisement ben't his fate,
Gad's curse! it may in time destroy the state.
I hold no one its friend, I must confess,
Who would discauntenance your men of dress.   10
Far, give me leave t'abserve, good clothes are things
Have ever been of great support to kings;
All treasons come from slovens, it is nat
Within the reach of gentle beaux to plat;
They have no gall, no spleen, no teeth, no stings,   15
Of all Gad's creatures, the most harmless things.
Through all recard, no prince was ever slain
By one who had a feather in his brain.
They're men of too refined an education,
To squabble with a court—for a vile dirty nation.   20
I'm very pasitive you never saw
A through republican a finished beau.
Nor, truly, shall you very often see
A Jacobite much better dressed than he.
In shart, through all the courts that I have been in,   25
Your men of mischief—still are in faul linen.
Did ever one yet dance the Tyburn jig,
With a free air, or a well-powdered wig?
Did ever highwayman yet bid you stand,
With a sweet bawdy snuff-bax in his hand?   30
Ar do you ever find they ask your purse
As men of breeding do?—Ladies, Gad's curse!
This author is a dag, and 'tis not fit
You should allow him ev'n one grain of wit:
To which, that his pretence may ne'er be named,   35
My humble motion is,—he may be damned.

FINIS

22 *through* thorough-going
27 *dance*   jig at the rope's end